The Clint Wilkes Original College Guide to a Summer Job In Yellowstone

The Clint Wilkes Original
COLLEGE GUIDE TO A SUMMER JOB IN YELLOWSTONE

by Clint Wilkes

On the back cover: top photograph, left to right, Matthew, Lancaster Theological Seminary, Katie, Sweet Briar College, Shane, U. of Alabama, Dee, Ohio State, and Christina from U.C. Santa Barbara. Lower left, Wendy from Maryland, and right, Chantal from Auburn.

Copyright © 1994 by Clint Wilkes. This book, "THE CLINT WILKES ORIGINAL COLLEGE GUIDE TO A SUMMER JOB IN YELLOWSTONE", is copywrited material belonging solely to Clint Wilkes.

Clint Wilkes Publishing Company
ALL RIGHTS RESERVED.

We are delighted for reviewers and writers of magazine and newspaper articles to quote passages from this book as needed for their work. Otherwise, no part of this book may be reproduced or transmitted in any form or by any means, electronic or mechanical, including photocopying, recording or by any information storage and retrieval system, without written permission of the publisher.

ISBN 0-9641435-0-X

All photos by Clint Wilkes

To obtain copies of this book by mail, please send $12.95 plus $3.00 shipping and handling, total $15.95 per copy to:

Clint Wilkes Yellowstone Guide
P.O. Box 192
Pinson, Alabama 35126

This book is dedicated to my two
god-daughters, April and Bonnie.

I would like to extend a special THANK YOU to my sister-in-law, Joan. Her help in editing this work was invaluable. Any errors remaining are entirely mine.

THANKS TO:
Stephanie & Kim at T.W. Services
Nina at Hamilton
Hal at Y.P.S.S.
Marsha & Denny at N.P.S.
Susan & Bob at Interior
Captain Jackson at U.S.A.F.A.
Linda, Lori & David at The Court
Tom at the City of Austin
Colleen & Jessica at Lake Highland
Cory at University of Oklahoma
Maria CPA in 95
Lynda & Sam at Parkway
Misty at Texas Tech
Patsy at Ag
Frances at TEC
Wayne in Galveston
Tom & Betty in Newhouse
Catherine at S.M.U.
CoCo
Sheila in Arkansas
Amy and Donna in Louisiana
Ruth at N.E. Louisiana
Mom & Dad

Table of Contents

CHAPTER 1 - INTRODUCTION 1

CHAPTER 2 - TRACY GETS A JOB IN YELLOWSTONE 5

CHAPTER 3 - HELPFUL HINTS 9

CHAPTER 4 - EMPLOYERS & JOBS 25

CHAPTER 5 - OLD FAITHFUL 65

CHAPTER 6 - ROOSEVELT 87

CHAPTER 7 - LAKE YELLOWSTONE 103

CHAPTER 8 - MAMMOTH 109

CHAPTER 9 - GRAND CANYON OF THE YELLOWSTONE . . 117

CHAPTER 10 - GRANT VILLAGE 123

CHAPTER 11 - HIKING 127

CHAPTER 12 - WINTER IN YELLOWSTONE 133

CHAPTER 13 - WORKING NEAR YELLOWSTONE 139

CHAPTER 14 - MEAN PEOPLE SUCK! 147

CHAPTER 15 - ANIMALS 155

CHAPTER 16 - THE FIRES OF '88 165

CHAPTER 17 - MY SUMMER 169

CHAPTER 18 - THE AUTHOR 175

The Clint Wilkes Original College Guide to a Summer Job in Yellowstone

Introduction

Most of the time when you consider how to spend your Summer, your choices would probably be watching Chuck connect the couples or watching Vanna turn the letters. Unfortunately most parents do not understand the value you place on these learning experiences. They want you to "get a job."

After a tough year at college, where you spent all your spare time studying, you want to relax. A job in Yellowstone will not be relaxing. They do expect you to perform your duties, but it will be more fun than you can imagine, and the adventure of a lifetime. You will have plenty of time off to explore the Park or do whatever you want. The best part is, there are no finals.

In the past most of the people who found out about

jobs in Yellowstone were people who knew someone who had worked in the Park. Getting a job in Yellowstone has never been kept a secret, it has just not been publicized.

This book is intended to level the playing field and give you an equal opportunity to compete for a job in Yellowstone.

Why am I writing a book about jobs in Yellowstone and what makes me think you can get a job there? There is an easy answer but one most people, including me, did not think about, until now!

Yellowstone is in the "middle of no-where". I know the phrase "middle of no-where" is used in a lot of situations. This time we can prove it. Get out a map and locate the Park. It is mostly in the Northwest corner of Wyoming, with parts overlapping into Idaho and Montana. It really is in the "middle of no-where".

Here is a place with several million tourist visiting it each year. There are no major colleges or large cities close by. The employers must hire workers from whereever they can get them. This includes all over this country and even from foreign countries. There is no reason you could not be one of those.

If we were talking about summer jobs in Yosemite then we would be talking California with about a zillion college students within a couple of hours drive. These "locals" have a big geographic advantage toward working in Yosemite. The same holds true for the Everglades near Miami or the Smoky Mountains with the entire East Coast population at its door.

My thoughts are, who would want to work anywhere but Yellowstone? This book will explain why I feel this way.

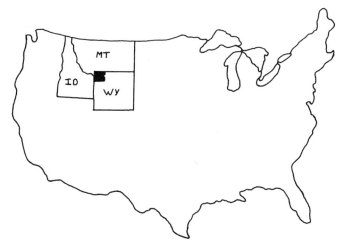

I have interviewed many of the several thousand college age Park employees. The vast majority think this was the best summer job they could ever have. A lot of students will work in Yellowstone more than one summer while they are in college.

It never occurred to me when I was going to College to try to get a Summer job in Yellowstone. Even today when I ask college students if they would like to work in the Park I get the same response! "Yes, what do I need to do?"

This book cannot guarantee you will get hired; however, it is going to tell you what you need to do to get an opportunity for a Summer job. It will tell where the jobs are and in general what you will be doing. I will talk about Winter jobs in a separate chapter.

◆◆◆

The Clint Wilkes Original College Guide to a Summer Job in Yellowstone

I am very fortunate to have friends in the Interior Department and the National Park Service to vouch for my credibility. They gave me introductions to the Yellowstone Concessionaires.

T.W. Recreation Services, Hamilton Stores Inc., and Yellowstone Park Service Stations were helpful in every way.

At no time did I conduct any interview with a college student in the presence of their Supervisor. The concessionaires also did not approve, disapprove or discuss with me any questions I might ask during interviews.

I was the sole judge of the appropriateness of all interviews.

My only concern was to get an accurate view of what it is like to work for a summer in Yellowstone.

You are the judge of my endeavor.

◆◆◆

Here are a few words which I will use a lot.

TOURON is a tourist who does something dumb. **Never** use this word in front of anyone.

T.W. is T.W. Recreational Services.

Hamilton is Hamilton Stores Inc.

Y.P.S.S. is Yellowstone Park Service Stations.

The Pub is the bar for all Park employees. All locations except Roosevelt have a Pub. For Roosevelt Pub information, ask a Wrangler.

E.D.R. is the Employee Dining Room.

Scat is what bears do anywhere and anytime they want.

Tracy Gets A Job In Yellowstone

Ever since my first trip to Yellowstone I have encouraged college students to spend their summers working in Yellowstone. Here is the story of the first person I "suggested" contact T.W.SERVICES, the Park's largest employer, and apply for a Summer job in Yellowstone.

I talked with a friend after my second trip to Yellowstone. She had a daughter named Tracy, a first year student at a local college. Tracy loved animals and worked part-time as an assistant to a Veterinarian. During my trip I had noticed all the college-age employees working all over the Park. It occurred to me Tracy would probably enjoy working in Yellowstone. When I got home I talked to Tracy about the possibility, and she thought it was a great idea. All I could tell her then was to write a letter to T.W. Services and get an application. She did write to request an application and got it within a few days. She filled it out and returned it. A couple of months later she received an acceptance letter saying she had been hired to work in Activities Sales at Roosevelt Lodge. (The jobs will be explained in detail later.)

One thing I need to mention is Tracy loves her Mother very much and even though she was thrilled at the thought of working in Yellowstone, she was terrified of being over a thousand miles from home. We must remember she was nineteen and had never been away for more than a weekend at her Dad's. Her Mom and I assured her she could come home any time she wanted if she did not like it. I must admit I even tossed in a bribe of a gift certificate to *The Gap* if she would at least go for a few days and give the Park a chance. Tracy departed, crying, about noon. She arrived in Bozeman, Montana later that afternoon. When she called us from the airport, she was still crying.

We had arranged transportation for her to a hotel about thirty miles east of Bozeman in Livingston, Montana. There she would be picked up the next morning and bussed the fifty miles to T.W. headquarters. The T.W. offices are near the Parks Northern entrance in Gardiner, Montana.

Tracy called us from the hotel after she checked in. This time she was crying for two reasons. First, because she missed her mother; second, because she thought the room was a "dump". You must realize this is a hotel in Montana and even though it was very clean and comfortable it was, shall we say, "well worn". Tracy went on to call us five more times that night, her crying more sad with each call.

I tried to talk her into going to the restaurant and having dinner. She preferred to stay in her room, order room service and cry. She assured me she would give the Park a try. She also assured me we could expect her home real soon.

Tracy is a truly wonderful person. She has the type of personality which attracts people to want to be near her. She is usually smiling and happy. (Except when she is crying about missing her Mom and being in a "dumpy" hotel room.) Her Mom said she had always been a very happy person, even as a child.

Tracy called that night, for the fifth and last time, about midnight. She promised us she would call again the next morning before she boarded the bus.

I made sure I was at her Mom's house for that phone call because I was very concerned about her. Her Mom and I both picked up a phone extension when it rang. The voice I heard was the Tracy I knew so well, all laughs and happy. She told us she could only talk for a second. She had made some friends at breakfast and they were in a hurry to get seats together on the bus.

We did not hear from Tracy for the next three days! We called Roosevelt Lodge and left her a message to call us. She called that night and told us she was having the best time of her life!

Later in the summer we went to Yellowstone to see Tracy and to again visit the Park. I got to meet a lot of her friends. I was very impressed by the type of young person attracted to work in Yellowstone. Many of these friends would later come to visit her at home.

Tracy did have a wonderful Summer in Yellowstone and worked there again the next summer. Tracy was so anxious to return the second summer that she had her airline flight scheduled for two hours after her last final.

The employee Pub at Old Faithful

Helpful Hints

A Summer job in Yellowstone offers the opportunity for a lot of fun. Yellowstone is also a place with a lot of opportunity for danger. You are in a wilderness, never far from the bears and other animals. If you use common sense and follow the guidelines in the Park Ranger brochures, you should have a safe Summer.

◆◆◆

Todd from Maine is a perfect example of someone playing it smart. Todd worked at Old Faithful and had spent his off day in Cooke City, Montana. He was returning to the Park well after midnight when nature called. Todd stopped at the restroom facilities at Roosevelt. All went well until Todd stepped out the door of the men's room. A big bear had ambled out of the woods and was standing between Todd and his truck. Todd made what was both a wise and easy decision. He stayed put!

During the next hour he kept looking out the door and could see the bear was also staying put! After another hour Todd noticed the bear was asleep. He knew there was no way to get to his truck without going near the bear. He could only imagine the animal being as grouchy as his college roommate were he to wake the bear up.

Nights in Yellowstone can get very chilly. Todd had not paid any attention to the temperature until he realized he was probably going to be there for the rest of the night. Todd was dressed in the unofficial uniform of the off duty Park employee: shorts, T-shirt and hiking boots.

As the chill settled in, Todd studied the situation and made a discovery which kept him warm the rest of the night. Todd discovered the hot air handdryer on the wall. Todd made himself as comfortable as he could on the floor near the dryer and would turn it on whenever he felt cold. Todd stayed warm and safe and dozed off around 3:30. He awoke about 5:00 to discover the bear had departed.

Todd did exactly what you are suppose to do, which is report all bear sightings to the Park Rangers. The next several nights a Park Ranger was assigned to keep a lookout to see if the bear would return. Since it did not return, the Park Rangers assumed the bear was not going to establish a pattern of coming into the Roosevelt area each night.

Always remain on the lookout. A bear can be anywhere at any time and not all restrooms have the hot air handdryers!

◆◆◆

LODGING

Let's talk in general about the six lodging areas within the Park. In separate chapters on each area we will look at more specifics of that location. Several of these areas alone hold enough beauty to be a reason for a National Park and to visit Yellowstone.

Yellowstone has several camping areas within the Park.

Guess which lodging area is the most popular? You are correct, it is **Old Faithful.**

My favorite place in the Park is **Roosevelt.** This is where Roosevelt Lodge is located. Roosevelt is the smallest lodging area, but it has what I feel is the most "outdoorsy" atmosphere. I have taken my nephew, John, to Yellowstone twice. The first time when he was ten, then again last summer when he was twelve. He is already talking about what he will do when he works summers in the Park. He wants to work at Roosevelt.

The Lake Yellowstone area is beautiful! This area is usually referred to as **Lake**. This is the highest altitude lake in the United States. The Lake is gorgeous, and the water is always cold. I'll discuss the Bald Eagles later, in the chapter on Lake Yellowstone. The hotel at Lake is Five-Star. You may see a Movie Star or Congressman in the lobby.

The area with the Grand Canyon of the Yellowstone is referred to as **Canyon**. Once you have seen the Grand Canyon of the Yellowstone you will never forget it.

Mammoth Hot Springs is simply called **Mammoth.** This area is most noted for the colorful limestone terraces. They are covered in hot streams of water bubbling up from the earth.

Grant is located off the West Thumb of Yellowstone Lake. It is the newest location, built in the mid 1980s.

◆◆◆

DRIVING IN YELLOWSTONE

The main summer road in the Park is about 150 miles long, shaped kind of like a figure 8. It is called the GRAND LOOP ROAD. The top loop is called UPPER LOOP and the bottom loop is called LOWER LOOP. There are several small side roads off the loop roads. The loop road and the side roads will take you close to almost all the major attractions.

Vehicles of all kinds are prohibited from leaving the roads inside the Park. The most important reason is the disturbance this could cause to the animals. Also, serious permanent damage could be done to the habitat if cars, trucks, or motorcycles ventured off the road.

Most of the people driving in the Park are experiencing Yellowstone for the first time. If it is their first day in the Park and they see a buffalo or elk way off in the distance, they will slam on the brakes and grab the camcorder. It will take them a few days to realize they will definitely have an opportunity to view these animals from a safe and close distance. Elk and buffalo are a common sight all over the Park. By the time the tourist understand this their vacation is over.

Be very aware of tourists driving in the Park. They will always do the unexpected. They will stop, pull out in front of you, back into you and, in general, drive crazy! My favorite is the one who passes you then stops in front of you!

I was behind one of the many big camper vans one day. It plowed into the back of a car which had pulled out in front of it and unexpectedly stopped. The passenger in the car was thrown out the door she was opening to re-shut because she had not closed it securely. Her husband had come to a complete and sudden stop for this. The woman was badly bruised with nothing broken, but she could have been killed!

Also, this accident was the camper driver's fault because he hit them in the rear.

If you do see someone giving a turn signal, watch out! This does not mean they are going to either turn in that direction or even in the other direction. A turn signal should tell you only that something is about to happen.

Road work can only be done in Yellowstone during the brief summer. Winter conditions are too harsh to repair the roads. Plan on being delayed by road construction sometimes during your summer. Only Tourons get upset with road repairs!

In the winter, snowmobiles must also stay on the parts of the loop roads the Park Service has groomed for snowmobiling. Even though snowmobiles cause stress on the animals, you can still see evidence of snowmobile tracks where some dummy has ridden off the groomed road to get a better view of an animal.

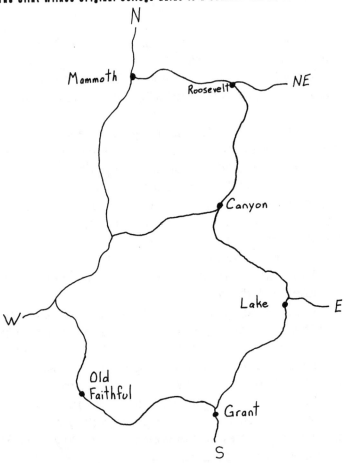

The Grand Loop

◆◆◆

FIVE ENTRANCES

The Park has five entrances open in the Summer.

Three of the entrances, **West, North** and **Northeast,** have small tourist towns located near the entrance gate.

Of the two other entrances, one to the **East** leads to Cody, Wyoming, about sixty miles away. There are several ranches with complete tourist facilities located near this entrance.

Cody has a rodeo each night. The rodeo and the Buffalo Bill museum in Cody are "must see" things to do at least once during your summer.

The **South** entrance adjoins the twenty miles of the Rockefeller Memorial Highway, which leads to Grand Teton National Park. You can go this route to drive the seventy miles to Jackson Hole, Wyoming. This is a real fun place; you will **definitely** be going to Jackson Hole!

You can also drive to Jackson Hole through the West entrance. This is where the town of West Yellowstone, Montana is located. Most people just say West when they refer to the town of West Yellowstone. To drive to Jackson Hole via West takes you a few miles into Idaho. Then you drive south about ninety miles, turn east twenty miles directly over the Grand Tetons into Jackson Hole.

Five miles from the North entrance is Mammoth Hot Springs. You will refer to this area as Mammoth. The town of Gardiner, Montana is located at this Park entrance.

The North entrance is the entrance where the giant arch is located. The arch has "For The Benefit And Enjoyment Of The People" inscribed on top. It was dedicated by President Teddy Roosevelt.

There are a lot of stories about how the children's stuffed animal bear got the name *"Teddy"* bear. My favorite is the one where President Roosevelt was hunting outside Yellowstone and would not shoot a Mother Bear because it had a baby bear with her. The press reported the story nationwide. Hence the name *"Teddy"* was associated with small bears and toy manufacturers were quick to describe their stuffed children's bears as

"Teddy" Bears.

About fifty years ago, foresters rescued an injured small bear from a fire. They kept the bear as a mascot, naming it *"Hot Foot Teddy"*. As the story of the rescue spread across the country, some smart P.R. person changed the mascot's name to what we now call, "Smokey Bear".

Today they will put you under the jail if they catch you hunting bears or any animal in the Park.

My favorite *Teddy* Bear is inside the Old Faithful Inn. To see this *Teddy* Bear, do this: Stand in front of the fireplace about ten steps, stand facing the front door. Look to almost the top of the ceiling of the pole in the left center. Now you can see where construction workers left a small *Teddy* Bear over twenty years ago. I tried to photograph this, but the photograph did not show the *Teddy* very well. It's hard enough to see in person.

The fifth entrance is the Northeast entrance. It is located about fifteen miles from Roosevelt Lodge. Here, outside the Park, there are two towns. Silver Gate, Montana is only a few blocks from the entrance. Then four miles down the road is Cooke City, Montana.

This is the route to the city of Red Lodge, Montana. The road between Cooke City and Red Lodge is called the Beartooth Highway. This road does not open til well into June. I strongly suggest you take the route via Livingston to get to Gardiner if you drive to the Park. You will want to visit Red Lodge, Montana at least once during the Summer. Be prepared for the most winding road you have ever seen. The drive alone is worth the trip to Red Lodge. It's about fifty miles from Cooke City and takes about two hours to drive.

◆◆◆

Bring a whistle and always wear it around your neck. This may sound like the silliest thing you have ever heard, but you are never more than several steps from the wilderness. A whistle works a lot better than yelling when you wander off and are lost in the woods.

Actually, carrying a whistle will not sound as silly as my next suggestion. When you go hiking you will want to put bells on your backpack and your walking stick. On a hike you DO WANT TO MAKE NOISE! When you are hiking, as much as you may try, it is difficult to maintain constant conversation. Now would be a good time to be with that friend who will never shut up. Bells on your walking stick and backpack will make noise. Normally bears and other animals will avoid any noises they hear approaching.

◆◆◆

In a backpack there is one essential item to carry besides your bells: toilet paper. If it is an "emergency" and you must use one of the stand alone restrooms, it is possible it will not have TP. Before you leave home, pick up some of the small travel-size TP packets. They are available at almost all grocery or drug stores.

Carry your own TP! It is terribly rude to borrow from someone else. They may not need it now, but they will need it.

If at all possible, wait to use an inside restroom in one of the lodging areas.

◆◆◆

Buy some good hiking boots. You will want to go hiking and Yellowstone hikes require good hiking boots for comfort.

◆◆◆

Pack lightly. You will have one or two roommates. There are places for employees to wash their clothes free, so you can bring a few outfits and wash them when needed. You can always have more clothes sent to you.

The off duty unofficial uniform of the Park employee is a combination of whatever you have clean (or almost clean) to wear. Yellowstone has no fashion police! I assure you no one cares what anyone wears.

I also suggest a good sleeping bag designed for cold weather. Do not bring your little brothers old Ninja Turtle sleeping bag.

You need to be aware of the weather in Yellowstone. It has been known to snow in June, July and August. Even on a warm day it can get chilly at night, so you will need some warm clothes. The weather in the Park can also change from sunshine to rain in a hurry.

Several years ago Yellowstone had a blizzard on August 25. The Park employees and guests visiting the Park were stuck where they were—so they had a Christmas Party. Since then, every August 25, they have an employee Christmas Party in the Park, complete with a Christmas tree.

The Christmas tree is in a unique and special location near the geyser area. Senior Park employees will get together and choose among themselves two people to go late at night on August 24, "Christmas" eve, to decorate the tree. It is against Park rules to put ornaments and other decorations on trees. So far the Park employees have not been caught. The Park Rangers must clean the decorations from the tree. This is done soon after

The Clint Wilkes Original College Guide to a Summer Job In Yellowstone

'Christmas' is over. They always have many volunteers for this job because the Park employees always leave a case of beer under the tree for the Ranger clean up crew.

All of these weather changes have a meteorological explanation about Yellowstone being on a plateau and the Pacific coastal winds. All of this means nothing if you get wet and cold, so bring a raincoat and sweater and keep them close.

All over the Park you will see small restrooms standing alone. Some will be unisex and some will have a separate women's and men's facility. Do not use these unless it is a major "emergency". They smell bad on their best day and if it is a hot summer day without wind...well, I warned you.

.....well, I warned you.

The Clint Wilkes Original College Guide to a Summer Job In Yellowstone

There are workers who get fired. You can be fired if you are late to work five times. If you call to let your supervisor know you will be late, it will not count as one of the five times. (Unless you are abusive in calling in late.)

◆◆◆

Yellowstone is located at a very high elevation. You should check with your Doctor before arriving to be sure the high altitude will not affect your health.

◆◆◆

Do not bring your pet unless you want it to be a coyote snack. (Anyway, employee pets are not allowed.)

◆◆◆

The next topic is an area I have done absolutely no research on. Yellowstone is a lot like your college campus. You have several thousand women and men living and working close together. I would guess the romance situation you encounter in the Park will be the same as your campus. Your behavior in the Park offers the same risk of Aids and STDs as anywhere.

Yellowstone does have one different aspect for you to remember. Bears are attracted to sexual activity. I am not going to explain why, but it is true. It is even in some of the Park Ranger brochures.

◆◆◆

The Clint Wilkes Original College Guide to a Summer Job in Yellowstone

If there is someone weak enough to use drugs, I hope they do not want to work in Yellowstone. Of course, the world is full of weak people, so they need to be advised. Yellowstone is Federal property. If you get caught using drugs, I am certain you will be immediately fired. You also will face charges, not from some local police municipality, like your campus or home town, but from the Federal Government.

In many cases a drug user will inadvertently turn themselves in to the Rangers. This was the case with one college lady we will call Diane. (not her real name.)

Diane was in her dorm room smoking a joint. She looked out the window and what she saw was three guys kicking a rabbit. Diane leaned out her window and yelled at them to quit kicking the rabbit. They ignored her and continued what they were doing.

Diane then went to the phone in the hall and dialed the Rangers at 911. She told them there were three guys out in the parking lot kicking a rabbit around. Diane told the dispatcher she had yelled at them to quit but they had ignored her.

The Rangers will respond to all emergencies at once. They will respond especially quick to a report of someone abusing an animal.

Within two minutes, four different Ranger police cars were pulling into the parking lot of the dorm. They completely surrounded the three guys. One guy was getting off a perfect kick as the first Ranger car approached.

Ian, from Texas, plays soccer for Davidson College. The soccer ball travelled in a straight line for twenty yards where Eric, who starts Ohio Medical School in Toledo in August, made a perfect kick over to Jason, who graduated from North Carolina State.

The Rangers walked over to Ian, Jason and Eric and

asked if anyone had been yelling at them. Before they could answer, a Hamilton store manager, who had been working on his car near the soccer players, told the Ranger he had heard a girl on the second floor yelling at the boys, "stop kicking the rabbit".

Diane had given her real name, which is not Diane, and room number to the 911 dispatcher. The Rangers went up to her room. They could smell pot from three doors down.

Diane was busted and fired on the spot!

Diane was given eight hours to have her belongings out of the dorm. The fine was almost eight hundred dollars, which the federal judge allowed Diane to pay at fifty dollars per month.

◆◆◆

This book is not a guide on how to become a Park Ranger. Within the Park Service, working in Yellowstone is considered one of the "primo" jobs. Ranger Dan Sholly, the Parks Chief of Rangers, actually took a pay cut to work in the Park. He has an excellent book, *"Guardians Of Yellowstone"* about his job and a Ranger's perspective on Yellowstone. To get an application to be a Park Ranger, contact the National Park Service in Washington D.C. ◆◆◆

Geologists have a lot of explanations on the formation of Yellowstone. They talk about calderas and volcanos. My theory on how Yellowstone was formed goes like this: Summer and Winter were talking one day and they made a bet on who could create the most beauty in Yellowstone. They tied!

This book is intended for those of you who want the adventure of a lifetime set in the world's most beautiful place.

Here are the addresses and phone numbers for the three companies you will need to write or call for an application for a job in Yellowstone.

T.W. Recreational Services
Employment Office
P.O. Box 165
Yellowstone Park, Wyoming 82190
Phone 307-344-5324

◆

Yellowstone Park Service Stations
P.O. Box 11
Gardiner, Montana 59030
Phone 406-848-7333

◆

Hamilton Stores Inc. has two addresses:
From April 1 til Oct. 31 mail to:
P.O. Box 250
West Yellowstone, Montana 59758
Phone 406-646-7325
OR
Hamilton Stores Inc.
From Nov. 1 til March 31 mail to:
1709 West College
Bozeman, Montana 59715
Phone 406-587-2208

◆

To Contact the PARK RANGERS in Yellowstone
DIAL 911
or 307-344-7381

Employers & Jobs

The jobs in the Park are not gender related. In all my trips to Yellowstone I have seen women performing every task. I encourage more women to apply to work in all the jobs in the Park.

To get an application, call or write the company you are interested in. Their addresses and phone numbers are at the end of chapter three. They will mail you an application. When you fill out the application, be accurate. These companies do check out prospective employees. References are very important. I would guess putting your parole officer as a reference would not move your name to the top of the list.

◆◆◆

Different facilities within the Park open and close at different times. The opening and closing dates will be in your application or you can call to get exact dates.

You will be asked what dates you can work. This will be part of your "work agreement". It is important you are accurate concerning your dates to be available to work.

A lot of colleges are now starting and ending their school year at times much different than in the past. You may be able to work at the beginning or end of the summer. The companies need employees every day, so you may be able to get a job even if you are only available for a short time. These jobs are not "rocket science" and most are quickly learned.

After you mail in your application, you may receive a letter offering you a job or you may get a phone call in which they will conduct a telephone interview. If they call to interview you, turn the MTV off, not just down. You may also pre-plan to have your roommate do like Elvis and leave the building. This is an important phone conversation. This is a summer in Yellowstone!

Once they decide to offer you a job they will do it by mail. This letter will contain details of the job they offer plus a work agreement for you to sign. The work agreement is very important. It will state specifically the dates of your employment. These companies are counting on you to fulfill your obligation.

In Yellowstone, you will work a five day week. Your two off days will be in succession. Everyone refers to their two off days as their "weekend". The days could be any two days of the week. Once you get there you will notice little difference in the days of the week.

You may be asked or even required to work on your

off days if unusual circumstances occur.

If you have not received a letter offering you a job within six weeks of mailing your application, call them. There could be a delay in sending job offers or they are not going to offer you a job. They will tell you which category you are in.

If you are not offered a job now, you can call later in the summer and check on jobs available. If you're not hired, forget it. This is a great summer job, but it is still just a summer job. (Especially don't get mad at me.)

The Concessionaires are in Yellowstone upon the approval of the United States Congress. From my observations, these companies do exactly what Congress has authorized them to do. If you have a problem with any of these companys then you should contact your Member of Congress.

All of the employers in Yellowstone will treat you like the adult you are. Unfortunately, some people do not want to act like an adult. They all will fire you for "just" cause!

My observations and my conversations with employees led me to conclude most supervisors are fair with employees. You will always have personality conflicts any time you put several thousand people together. All of these companies encourage you to contact the Personnel Department to report any activity you do not feel is appropriate.

I only met one "jerk" management person during my summer. See the chapter *"Mean People Suck"*.

Here are the three companies to work for in Yellowstone.

T.W. RECREATIONAL SERVICES

The largest employer within the Park is a mega-corporation called T.W. RECREATIONAL SERVICES. They are a division of a big conglomerate somewhere. If you just say "T.W." or "T.W. Services"; everyone will know what you mean. They manage the lodging and a lot of the restaurants and souvenir stores. Your first choice for a company to work for in Yellowstone will most likely be T.W. I feel most of the college students who work for them agree they are treated well.

T.W. makes a bundle off the Park as they have exclusive rights over a lot of what is sold inside the Park. I've always been satisfied with my dealings with T.W. At least it's American owned. Several years ago the Japanese actually bought the company running Yosemite. After a stink was raised our Government made them sell it off to an American owned company.

T.W. hires about seventy percent of the Parks college Summer workers. Most of the T.W. jobs require a degree of physical exertion which can easily be performed by most college students. I'm talking about various jobs like making beds and waiting tables, not digging ditches.

◆◆◆

Y.P.S.S. hires mostly college students. Women perform the task of changing flat tires and oil changes as easily as men.

◆◆◆

Hamilton hires about three or four hundred college students. They will work as COOKS, WAITSTAFF, or as GROCERY CLERKS, plus many other positions.

◆◆◆

As I describe the jobs you will easily understand the physical capacity required.

T.W. Jobs

I will mention some of the jobs now to give you an idea of the different jobs. I will also mention other jobs when I discuss the different areas in the Park. I will CAPITALIZE all jobs at least once in this book. If you see one you would be interested in you can request it. Put as much supporting reference information as you can gather to help you get the job. Let them know if this is the only job you will accept or if it is just your first choice.

About twenty percent of the T.W. employees are full time, year round. I met many of these when I spent a month during the Winter in Yellowstone working on my WINTER chapter. These are some of the most interesting people you will ever meet.

Janell, a wrangler from Hocking College in Ohio.

The most "glamorous" jobs in the Park are the WRANGLERS and the COACH DRIVERS. These are the people working with the horses, wagons and stagecoaches.

You must be very good with horses to get one of these jobs. I saw a lot of women Wranglers and Coach Drivers on my many trips to the Park. In the old days the word Cowboy might have been used to describe this job. Today women perform the task as easily as men, so Wrangler seems very appropriate. Wranglers work with horses, mainly leading horseback tours. The Coach Drivers drive the stagecoaches and wagons. You had better be real good with horses to even think about one of these jobs. To apply call T.W. and set up a phone interview with one of the Head Wranglers at the corrals at Roosevelt, Canyon or Mammoth. The phone number for T.W. is 307-344-5324.

If you work in Roosevelt, Canyon or Mammoth you will be around horses a lot. These are the areas with the corrals for horse activities. What I am about to tell you is something you will learn real quick once you get to the Park. Horses go to the bathroom a lot. To them a bathroom is where they happen to be standing at the time. There is an old saying used a lot by people who attend Polo matches and go on the field during the break to kick the divots back in place. "Do not kick a rock or divot if steam is coming off it."

Many of the jobs require you to stand all day. In addition to your hiking boots I strongly recommend good work shoes.

A popular job is GUEST SERVICE ASSISTANT. In this position you check people in and out and do basically the same thing a front desk clerk does at any hotel. If you are not a "people-person", do not request this job.

If you are a real "people person", even more than front desk job quality, then the perfect job is TOUR GUIDE. All kinds of different tours are offered every day. For some of these jobs you may need to know how to drive a minibus and need a special drivers license for the big busses. Lori, a Kent State grad has been a tour guide for several seasons. She had driven a student shuttle bus in College.

The National Park Service gives many narrative tours around the Park. These tours are conducted by Park Rangers.

◆◆◆

A STOREKEEPER at each location orders and controls the inventory for various hotels and restaurants.

If you are good with numbers, apply to be a CONTROLLER or AUDITOR. They "crunch the numbers" daily at each lodging facility. You do not have to be an Accounting Major to apply for these jobs.

Imagine getting paid to talk on the phone. Apply to work in RESERVATIONS. Over fifty people work during the Summer in the reservations office upstairs in the Mammoth Hotel. This can be a real fun job if you have a good boss. I was told Nels from California was the best to work for in past summers. (Nels is who told me this!)

This summer Nels was working as a VENDING ROUTE DRIVER in the Service Department. This involves driving a white van full of snacks around the Park, refilling all the vending machines. The van drivers work a long day and are usually on a tight schedule. They need a bumper sticker which says, "Don't Like My Driving— Dial 1-800-EAT-SCAT".

The Clint Wilkes Original College Guide to a Summer Job in Yellowstone

Dana worked in Reservations and also worked part-time at K-Bar

There is no doubt in my mind T.W. would fire the driver who put a bumper sticker like that on a van. (They would fire them only after they checked with their attorneys to see if they could legally hang the driver from a tree by their thumbs.)

A vending driver is one of the more fun jobs. There are four jobs available, and they are very difficult to get. You must know where every vending machine is located in the entire Park. Because of the short season, it would be difficult to learn all the locations in your first Summer in Yellowstone.

You can still work in the Service Department. Matthew was this summer's manager of the Service Department which includes Vending Drivers. Over twenty people work in this department. Some of the jobs are, working at Bridge Bay or Canyon as LAUNDRY ATTENDANTS. Near Bridge Bay and Canyon are camping sights. A large building has a laundry and showers. These jobs require you to collect money from the guests who want to take a shower and to sell laundry detergent for the self serve washers and dryers.

I met Matthew the day Lake Hotel opened. I had heard Nels was working in VENDING, and I saw a man from the back loading a vending machine. Having met him during the Winter I remembered Nels had a gigantic, unruly red beard. From the back I could see a beard, but this beard was well kept; it could not be Nels. I went up and introduced myself and met Matthew from Chicago. Matthew managed the Service Department. We talked for quite a while and even had lunch together. Matthew had started working in Yellowstone eight years prior as a DISHWASHER. Today he manages over twenty people.

My friend's daughter, Tracy, worked at Roosevelt in ACTIVITY SALES. There are Activity Sales offices all over the Park. This job consists of the sale of tickets for the various activities there are to do in the Park, such as horseback rides, boat rentals, tours, the Roosevelt Cookout and all the other fun events.

All of the activities I just mentioned also need employees.

The LAKE area needs DOCK HELP, FISHING GUIDES and SCENICRUISER GUIDES for the boat tours. If you are a qualified life guard, be sure to mention this if you want to work at Lake Yellowstone. It is not a requirement for all the jobs at Lake, but it could help you get the job.

I would think being a COOK/SERVER on the Roosevelt Cookout would be a fun job. This does not require you to be a French Chef. Most of the food is pre-prepared at the Lodge. Your main job would be setting up the food. The meal is self serve buffet style for most of the meal except a COOK/SERVER cooks and serves the steaks.

◆◆◆

T.W. has a fleet of vehicles to be maintained, and they service all of them in the Park. If you are qualified, apply to be a MECHANIC. Call T.W. and speak with the manager of the MECHANICS.

T.W. also needs DRIVERS to transport whatever needs transporting throughout the Park. You may drive a regular pick up truck or van or you may drive a larger vehicle which might require a special license. If you have a special license already be sure to let them know.

One of the best jobs for making money is WAITPERSON. Tips are where you earn extra income. Waiting tables in Yellowstone is basically the same as waiting tables anywhere. You have mostly good customers with a few rotten apples every now and then.

Not every person who does not leave a fair tip is necessarily a rotten apple. One day I had lunch at the Old Faithful Inn. To pay your check you take the bill up to the CASHIER. In front of me paying by credit card was an absolutely darling "little old couple". They were telling the cashier how sweet their waitress had been. They said she reminded them of their great-granddaughter. As they handed their money to the cashier they looked back towards their table and saw a BUSSER cleaning the table. The lady, with a real sound of concern in her voice, told the cashier they had left the tip in cash and were concerned the busser would abscond with the tip. The cashier, in a most calm manner, assured the lady theft was not a problem and, yes indeed, the correct person would receive the tip. The older lady looked relieved and said, "Our waitress did such a wonderful job I would hate for her to not get that QUARTER we left." The cashier remained straight-faced and once again assured her all would be taken care of.

A few days later I drove down to the Grand Tetons with Cathy, a school teacher tourist from Missouri. I met Cathy her last day in the Park. Her flight was out of Jackson Hole late that afternoon. I offered her a ride to the airport, and we planned to stop at Jackson Lake Lodge for lunch.

We did not get to the Lodge till after the main dining room had closed for lunch. I was very disappointed because the view of the Tetons from the main dining room is magnificent.

We proceeded to the adjacent eating area, a rather nifty fifties style diner, all with revolving seats at a very long and meandering counter. No booths or tables, only counter seating.

Our wait-person was Jennifer from Pennsylvania. Like I had done on every previous encounter with a Park employee, I told her I was writing a book about the employees of Yellowstone and was also going to mention the employees of The Grand Teton Lodge Company.

Jennifer said, "big deal, I could care less". I loved it, she reminded me of my favorite burger place in Austin. *GMs* was on the Drag across from the UT campus. The wait staff was always snarly and would squirt a fake bottle of ketchup on you if you asked a dumb question, like asking for extra mayo. They would say "no", then squirt the bottle which released a string which looked like a stream of ketchup. They were always funny and no one ever got upset ("Progress" closed GM's over the summer.).

Jennifer would be a perfect *GM* employee. I could

tell she was only having fun with her statements. We talked and laughed with Jennifer for quite a while. She told us how she had been planning to work in the Tetons for two years. A friend had told her about the job then, and she had saved the phone number that entire time.

I remembered the "little old couple" as Jennifer handed me our check to take up to the register to pay. I looked at her and said, "Jennifer, you have been such a great waitress I am going to add a quarter tip to my credit card." Jennifer looked back at me and said, "thank you sir, now I can get that heart operation I need to stay alive."

I went back for lunch several more times and always requested Jennifer. Each time, just like that first time, I would put a five dollar tip on what was usually a ten dollar lunch.

◆◆◆

In the kitchen you can also be a COOK or COOK'S HELPER. A really rotten job is DISHWASHER, but a lot of people are willing to take the rotten jobs to be in Yellowstone.

If you do get a rotten job, you can request a transfer. Just do a good job and you can get transferred. I talked to a lot of college people who worked as a dishwasher for one or two weeks, then moved. Do your job and do not be afraid to ask for a transfer!

You can apply to be a BUSSER. They set and clean up the tables. This was the job I always tried to get when I was on K.P. in the Army. (I never got a single tip.)

You can serve as a HOST/HOSTESS in the dining rooms.

Several people told me the best job is BELL PORTER. This job entails unloading luggage and taking it to the guest rooms. The best part of this job is a lot of the Tours coming into the Park have pre-tipped as part of their tour package price. This is good news because a waitperson or a bell porter can get stiffed on a tip just as easily in Yellowstone as anywhere.

I saw Matt from Pittsburgh, a Bell Porter at the Old Faithful Inn a lot. He always had a great story to tell. I enjoyed talking with him each time. Matt is one of the most respected friends many employees have.

Mark, a Bell Porter at Lake, was also interesting to talk with. Mark has been with T.W. for several years.

◆◆◆

The Four Seasons Deli and Ice Cream Shop, located across from the Snow Lodge, is where I met an incredibly gregarious young lady named Marie. Marie finished high school in December and will attend the University of Maryland in September.

Marie took the bus from Baltimore to Yellowstone. During a stop in Minneapolis she saw two other students. Marie is not shy! She approached them and asked if by chance they were going to work in Yellowstone. Kristi and Adam are both from Mississippi and, yes indeed, they were headed to the Park. Kristi is on a tennis scholarship at Birmingham Southern College in Alabama, and Adam attends Meridian Junior College in Mississippi. They describe their relationship this way: they have been "hanging out together" for over a year. They both work in the Old Faithful Lodge Cafeteria. Adam is a COOK. Kristi is a COLD LINE SERVER. This job requires her to keep all the cold foods on the cafeteria line stocked.

The "hanging out together" changed during mid summer. On a hike to Mystic Falls, Adam asked Kristi to marry him. She said "yes".

Dan, Adam, Kristi and the Author, somewhere in the wilderness.

I met Marie with my brief introduction and drew only the conclusion she was most likely a pleasant person. Little then did I realize how much help she would be to me during the summer. I saw her again in the Hamilton Store at Old Faithful a few days later on one of her off days. We had both bought apples and sat together on the front steps to eat. I had asked her if I could ask a few questions about her job and working in the Park. After a few minutes she asked if I wanted to see the employee dorms and other employee areas. Did I ever! I had only been in Yellowstone a few days and knew I would need to investigate these areas to have a complete book.

We first went to the employee laundry. At the start of each Summer, T.W. paints over all last year's graffitti and the new crew gets to make their own comments to the world on the wall. Marie is a writer and poet and was one of the first to leave her message. It was very good considering the location. The laundry is free and can only be used by T.W. employees. T.W. does expect you to keep your uniform clean. It's your option on how often you wash the sheets provided by T.W.

Our next venture was to Columbine Dorm. Marie showed me the dorm room she shared with Cheryl from Iowa. Some rooms have two people, some have three people. Columbine has women on the first floor, men on the second floor. Other dorms could have men and women on the same floor.

This was my second visit to a dorm room in over twenty years. Earlier in the school year I had visited April, my god-daughter's dorm room at S.M.U. That is where I took the cover photo.

About the only change in two decades is now you may see a PC on the desk. The only difference in Yellowstone is no one has a TV or radio because you cannot pick up any stations.

Everybody has at least some camping equipment. Marie is an avid hiker and had the works, external frame backpack, tent and "real" hiking boots. She left me reading more of her writing and went off to find people for me to meet. She returned within five minutes and led me to a room full of people sitting around listening to "Cher with Beavis and Butthead".

This was my first encounter with a lot of workers all together. They were all extremely bright and tried to be

One of several dorms at Old Faithful

helpful. They were also very funny. I was most impressed with one young man. He had said several things I wanted to follow up on. Meeting so many people at one time, it was impossible for me to remember anyone's name. Later, as Marie and I talked, I asked her the name of that particular person. She replied she did not know, she had only just met them when she was looking for people for me to meet.

I had met her the day the Four Seasons Deli opened. This was two days later, meaning she had only been in Yellowstone a few days. A week later I saw Marie again and she knew almost everyone in every dorm. She was always talking to any employee she would meet and was always a delight to be around.

Marie's job in the Four Seasons Deli had one gigantic drawback. This was the same drawback at all the ice cream shops operated by both T.W. and Hamilton Stores. The ice cream is hand-dipped and a lot of the cartons are frozen hard, which makes them difficult to dip. Wrist fatigue and wrist injuries are common. If possible the employees will alternate the dipping duty at the various locations. You could be on ice cream duty every day or every couple of days, depending on your location. I remember one day Marie told me she had been unable to brush her hair that morning after a previous day of ice cream dipping.

I did get to meet the person I had asked Marie about a few weeks later. Marie introduced me to Grant from New Jersey, and I found out a lot about working as a COOK'S HELPER.

GIFT SHOP CLERK is self-explanatory. This is a very popular job. Be sure to put any retail experience you have. They will check your references.

BARTENDER. You must be twenty-one. You can tend bar in either the guest bars or the employee Pub. The big drawback to working in the Pub is enforcing the twenty one age limit. You will always have someone who you know just graduated from high school try to pass off their fake I.D. Or someone over the legal age trying to buy drinks for one of his minor buddies. The Pub bartender can get fired for serving a minor even if it is by mistake!

Here is how I met Clark from Tennessee. Clark was the bartender at the Old Faithful Inn.

I had visited my older sister's four boys (Boys! The youngest is a Marine!) in North Carolina shortly before departing to spend my summer in Yellowstone. Jeff told me of his friend from Warren Wilson College who had

The Clint Wilkes Original College Guide to a Summer Job in Yellowstone

Clark from Tennessee, one of the "Good Guys" in Yellowstone

worked as a bartender the two previous summers in Yellowstone. As I left Jeff's house, I wrote his name on a slip of paper and it was lost before the day was out. I planned to call Jeff upon my arrival in the Park to get the name of his buddy.

While in the Old Faithful Inn, I meandered into the bar, hoping to find the mystery barkeep. The bartender at work had Clark from Tennessee on his name badge. I asked him if there were any bartenders from North Carolina. With a puzzled look on his face he said he was sort of from North Carolina, then his face brightened up and he said, "you must be Jeff's Uncle".

T.W. puts the name of your state of residence on your name badge. Clark is from Knoxville.

Clark is known by everyone as one of the "good guys". He is extremely likeable and fun to be around, even if you do not want to talk about fishing. Clark spends many of his off hours on Lake Yellowstone, fishing in the boat he keeps year round in Gardiner. (Actually it is a friend's boat...... possession is nine-tenths of the law.)

I enjoyed talking with Clark, but the biggest THANK YOU I want to give Clark is introducing me to *Eino's* Tavern. When I first met Clark he invited me to meet him and some friends at *Eino's* for dinner. *Eino's* will never be in "Architectural Digest".

Even with exact directions I drove past it. That could not be a place of business! I back-tracked and stopped

Clark wearing his favorite T-shirt.

at the only building in the area of Clark's directions. It was *Eino's*. It is seven miles north of West Yellowstone on highway 191. It is on the left just after the highway 287 exit.

I sat at the bar and told the bartender I was waiting on some friends to have dinner. I ordered my usual OJ and waited. *Eino's* is a small place, where you order your steak or chicken by ounces or you order a third pound or half pound burger. In the back is a large grill where you cook your own meal. The air in *Eino's* is heavenly, the aroma of all that cooking can make you suffer if you are starving and waiting on other folks for dinner.

The way *Eino's* is set up, I could see almost everyone in the place. I was setting at the bar with a giant pole beside me. I could see everyone except the person next to me on the opposite side of the pole. Clark had said to meet him about 7:30. I had arrived at 7:00. It was now 8:00 and he had not come through the front door. I could wait no longer, I had to have a half pound burger quick! I told the bartender I was ready to order. The unknown person on the opposite side of the pole plus the two women beside him were also ready to order. We got our plates of raw meat and all headed for the grill. I know you have already guessed Clark was the one person I could not see. We then proceeded to have dinner together.

Clark introduced me to his two friends and also to Jean, the bartender. Jean had married Ellert twelve years ago, six months after he had opened the tavern. *Eino's* is very popular with Park employees. It is open year round. I was a frequent customer all summer.

◆◆◆

Employees are needed to serve and cook for other employees in the Employee Dining Room (E.D.R.). The employees' Pubs at the various locations also need employees.

I was a guest in all of the E.D.R.s. You can only be a

guest in the E.D.R. a very few times. Guests must be escorted by an employee, sign in, and pay a nominal price for the meal. Later in the summer T.W. allowed me to eat in their E.D.R. for any meal. It would be difficult to say which E.D.R. was loudest. The food was good, but it was like eating with a jet taking off in your ear. (OK, I'm old. Most of the employees barely noticed the noise.)

It is very difficult to get permission for guests to visit the Pubs. The Pubs are available to all Park employees.

Employees are needed to be Managers and Custodians of the Employee Living Areas. (They do NOT clean your room.)

Elizabeth from Hollins College worked in Housekeeping at Canyon.

Some of the jobs do not sound like a lot of fun. Like jobs in HOUSEKEEPING!

T.W. hires a lot of students to work in the Housekeeping Department as ROOM ATTENDANTS. This involves cleaning the guests' rooms.

About ten percent of T.W. employees will quit before summer ends. About half of those work in Housekeeping. MOST of the employees may not like Housekeeping, but will stick out the job just because it is in Yellowstone.

There are also a lot of students who have been offered a job by T.W. as a room attendant, then do not show up in Yellowstone to work. This puts a tremendous work load on those Room Attendants who do arrive. If you are not going to show up after accepting the job, you need to call and let T.W. know.

I would guess after receiving the offer they find out what the job entails. The work is not fun. It involves changing sheets, vacuuming, and worst of all, cleaning bathrooms. I was told of one famous actor that stayed in the Park several years ago who never flushed the commode.

When a room attendant encounters an unflushed toilet, you may hear them call out, "sinking a battleship!"......Don't ask!

I cannot tell you whether you would hate being a room attendant or not. I met several students who had quit or been fired as room attendants. Yes, you can get fired from any job! If you cannot perform your duties you will be fired. About fifteen percent of employees get fired.

My investigation was not scientific. I discovered about fifteen percent of T.W. employees get fired and about ten percent quit. I would guess any C.E.O. in America would LOVE to have a seventy-five percent retention rate of employees, age eighteen to twenty-four.

The dreaded Housekeeping Cleaning Cart, near a cabin behind the Snow Lodge.

◆◆◆

I met Erich from the University of Louisville, who with his girlfriend, were room attendants at Mammoth. (Let me note, "girlfriend" was Erich's word. I would have put "woman friend" or "significant other".)

They both put on their applications they would work as Room Attendants if they could work together.

Like all of my first interviews with room attendants, I would wander around looking for a cleaning cart. I would approach, but **never** go into the room being cleaned. I would say hello to the room attendant and tell them I was writing a book about the people working in the Park. I would then chat briefly with them and hope I would see them again off duty somewhere. I did see almost everyone many times during the summer.

The one particular room attendant who seemed to be enjoying her job the most was Jenny from Grand Rapids Community College in Michigan. When Jenny first saw me she had on headphones and removed them to talk with me. Like so many of the women and men I met, Jenny loved Yellowstone. To her being a room attendant was a fair price to pay. As I was leaving I asked her what she was listening to. Her answer made my day! She was listening to "Janis Joplins Greatest Hits". When I was Jennys age, 19, I LOVED Janis Joplin. I was never in the drug scene, but I did love the music growing up in the 60s. Jenny let me borrow the tape a few days later. I kept it for a week and I must have played "Another Little Piece of My Heart" fifty times.

I'll now ask you the question I asked Jenny. Janis Joplin went to high school in Port Arthur, Texas with what currently famous person? Over the past few years I have asked a lot of people this. Jenny was the first to correctly say, "two time Super Bowl winning Coach Jimmy Johnson."

You most likely would have an excellent chance of getting hired if you requested a job as a ROOM ATTENDANT.

Room Attendants are assigned a number of rooms to clean. It should be easy to clean these during your eight hour shift. One problem is, when they are short of staff, everyone works till all rooms are clean. When they do have a full compliment of workers, if you finish early you can clock out. You only get paid for the hours you work. If you want to work a complete shift you can ask your supervisor for more work.

There are many other jobs available in housekeeping. These jobs involve everything from CLEANING CARPETS and doing the LAUNDRY to all the behind the scenes CLEANUP positions.

One job which is really not fun is working in the laundry in Gardiner. This is where all the hotels and cabins laundry are washed. To describe the place as hot and miserable would be more than fair! You can request a transfer. The turnover is high in the Gardiner Laundry.

All of the companies offer dorm lodging. Each location will have several dorms to house T.W. employees. T.W. trys to put the older workers in a dorm to themselves. With so many employees, this does not work at every location. Obviously the dorms with the most college age workers quickly gain a reputation as a "party dorm". The Park Rangers will make frequent visits to these dorms to check out funny smelling air, a federal offense in a National Park. T.W. and the National Park Service also strictly enforce the 21 age limit.

Do people under 21 drink? Do they drink on your campus?

HAMILTON STORES INC.

In 1915, Charles Hamilton became a concessioner in Yellowstone. Today HAMILTON STORES INC. is the oldest concessioner in the Park.

Hamilton Stores Inc. runs the GENERAL STORES and some of the food and souvenir shops in the Park. They hire college students and a lot of retired and older folks, usually married couples. The college students I have talked to say they really enjoy these Senior Citizens. I think part of this is the type of people who are attracted to work in the Park.

Nina Sims is one of the funniest and most fun people I have ever met! Nina is in charge of Human Resources for Hamilton Stores Inc. She was my liason to my meetings with many of Hamilton's college workers.

Hamilton was extremely easy to work with.

My interview with Nina consisted of over one hour of funny stories. Even though the stories were "G" rated, most of them ended with her saying, "please don't put that in your book."

Nina Sims should be a very good role model for women. She did not start college until she was forty. She graduated with Honors and has been an important player at Hamilton for several years.

◆◆◆

You could get a job working in a Hamilton Store, which are the General Stores within the Park. There are Hamilton Stores at all five lodging locations in the Park, plus several other locations. They need GROCERY CLERKS in the Grocery Department and they need SALES CLERKS to work the many other departments like photo, jewelry, gifts, etc.

Some of the Hamilton Stores have a GRILL and FOUNTAIN or a FAST FOOD OUTLET where they will need FOOD SERVICE CLERKS, FRY COOKS, KITCHEN or FOUNTAIN MAINTENANCE HELP, ICE CREAM SERVERS and KITCHEN and DINING ROOM ASSISTANTS.

Hamilton Stores Inc. also provides an E.D.R. (Employee Dining Room) and Employee Living Areas. These also need staff. I never heard of a Hamilton Dorm being a "party dorm". Also, the Hamilton E.D.R.s are mostly quiet. The food is served "family style".

Hamilton does not have any hotels in the Park, but they do operate the Branding Iron Motel and the Stagecoach Inn in West. You can apply to them for a Stagecoach Inn job which includes every position an Inn with TWO RESTAURANTS, a BAR and a GIFT SHOP would need.

Most employee lodging is located close to your work area.

The new employee lodging apartments located in West Yellowstone are first class. The only problem I have is the name of the apartment building. They are named "Buffalo Run". Long ago, Indians would stampede a herd of buffalo over a cliff to kill them for food. This was called a "buffalo run". (Nina Sims named it!)

At Fishing Bridge and Tower Falls Hamilton operates stores. The Tower Falls location has a GENERAL STORE complete with a gift shop, grocery department, microwave fast food and what has to be the busiest ice cream stand in Yellowstone. Even on cooler days the ice cream line would be long!

Fishing Bridge is one of the largest Hamilton Stores. It has a grill to cook burgers, etc. It also has a larger selection in every department.

YELLOWSTONE PARK SERVICE STATIONS

YELLOWSTONE PARK SERVICE STATIONS (Y.P.S.S) have seven GASOLINE SERVICE STATIONS in the Park. I

The Clint Wilkes Original College Guide to a Summer Job In Yellowstone

Alisa, from Towson State, cooking burgers at Fishing Bridge.

have been served by both women and men ATTENDANTS. They also have four first class GARAGES to work on guest vehicles. Qualified TECHNICIANS (mechanics) should call Y.P.S.S. to discuss the job and the pay. (406-848-7333)

Hal, the General Manager of Y.P.S.S., has both his Bachelor's and Master's Degrees from Auburn. (War Eagle!)

Steve from Montana has been the manager of Station Two at Old Faithful the past five years. He has worked for Y.P.S.S. for eight years. Station Two is next to the Hamilton Store near the Post Office. You can only get to this station via one route. It is a one way road and if you miss it you will never figure out how to get back.

I went into the Hamilton Store one morning to get my typical breakfast; chocolate milk, a banana and an apple. As I returned to my car I saw the dreaded flat tire. Luckily I was only a short distance from the Y.P.S.S. repair facility. I had enough air to drive without ruining my tire. I drove up and went in to tell Steve I was here to see him as a customer.

In a flash, Mike from Kansas repaired my tire. I think he completely missed my joke question of, "does the repair have a thirty-minute or thirty-mile warranty?" (Maybe he did not miss it and it was just not funny.)

Station One is beside the Old Faithful Inn and the other Hamilton Store. It has easy access and if you miss it you can easily return.

This station had four men and five women working at it. Three of the women have worked for Y.P.S.S. for several years. The other two are working their first summer. They all seem to love it! The day I met them they were covered in grease and having a great time.

Katie, from Tennessee, attends Sweet Briar College in Virginia and told me how one day she and three of the other women had gone out to a car that had pulled up to the full service pump. One pumped the gas, two cleaned the windows, and one checked the oil. The customer was one of her guy friends who worked at the Hamilton Store. She saw him the next day and he remarked on all the women around his car. He told Katie, "I thought I was in a beer commercial!"

Y.P.S.S. has many women working throughout the Park. Stephanie from Wellesley College just graduated. She worked all four summers in Yellowstone.

Matthew at Old Faithful Y.P.S.S.#1 recently graduated from Pennsylvania Seminary College. He already has a job lined up for the Fall. He will be working with a Christian organization called, "National Park Ministries". They work for Christian purposes in our National Parks.

◆◆◆

The Clint Wilkes Original College Guide to a Summer Job in Yellowstone

Matthew from Lancaster, Pennsylvania Seminary College.

A big fan of Hillary Rodham Clinton is Chas who is working her first summer at Y.P.S.S. at Fishing Bridge. Chas is from Arkansas and is proud of both Arkansas and the Clintons.

Chas goes to Hendrix College in Conway, Arkansas. When she told me this I asked her if she knew one of my favorite people, John Carpenter. John owns Coleman Office and School Supply in Conway. I always go to lunch with John any time I drive through Conway.

Chas said she did not know him but she had bought a lot of school supplies at his store.

◆◆◆

YELLOWSTONE PARK MEDICAL SERVICE

If you are interested in Medicine you may want to work with the YELLOWSTONE PARK MEDICAL SERVICE. They have summer needs for both professional and non-

The Clint Wilkes Original College Guide to a Summer Job in Yellowstone

Chas from Arkansas

professional personnel. The Park has a 24 HOUR EMERGENCY ROOM at the LAKE HOSPITAL, plus CLINICS at Old Faithful and Mammoth. This service in Yellowstone is provided through West Park Hospital in Cody, Wyoming.

If you took EMT courses be sure to let them know.
WEST PARK HOSPITAL
Attn: Yellowstone Park Medical Services
707 Sheridan Avenue
Cody, WY 82414
Phone (307)578-2461

◆◆◆

HELPFUL INFORMATION

How old do you have to be to get a job in Yellowstone? The minimum age varies with the different companies. T.W. is eighteen for most jobs. Hamilton

Stores Inc. and Y.P.S.S. have a nineteen age minimum for most of their jobs. The applications contain specific information.

◆◆◆

Each employer has rules. When you get your application it will give you the specifics. Most of the rules are "common sense".

◆◆◆

WHEELS

It is best to have your own car when you are working in Yellowstone. (Or make friends with someone who has a car, not a truck. Remember this, trucks can only carry one or two passengers inside and it can rain at any time.....which is not good if you are stuck riding in the back.)

The roads in Yellowstone vary between real bad and very bad. Only small sections of road are in excellent shape. If your first drive is in from West Yellowstone you will have the false impression all the roads are wonderful. You will quickly learn the truth. The winter conditions cause frost heaves and as much as they work on the roads, it is a no win battle. The Park Service tries to keep all the roads open during the summer. Sometimes a pot hole can get so big they may have to close off a section of the loop road for a short time or even a day or so to do repairs.

Road closure signs are posted at all the entrance gates.

If you drive carefully and keep an eye out for pot holes, you can avert some of them. You cannot avoid them all. I have run into several; one even broke part of my hubcap.

Buffalo have the "right of way" at all times in Yellowstone.

When I was a young sales rep a running joke was, "you can only take two kinds of vehicles into the backwoods of Colorado to go big game hunting, a four wheel drive truck and a company car."

Of course I never abused my company car, but I did hear of one rep who did. This rep was within a couple of weeks of reaching the mandatory mileage to trade in his company car for the latest model.

He and his buddy were going fishing in an area about two hundred miles from his home. They departed after work on Friday. Once they got about fifty miles out of town, they stopped at a convenience store to purchase two cases of their favorite beverage and two bags of ice.

As they pulled out of the parking lot they realized they had forgotten to buy an ice chest. The driver, realizing the urgency of the situation, made a quick and decisive move. He stopped the car, put the two cases of his favorite beverage in the backseat floorboard and poured the ice on top. They continued this procedure the rest of the weekend.

◆◆◆

GETTING THERE

You must furnish your own transportation to Yellowstone.

To get to the Park by airline, you may want to fly into West Yellowstone, Montana which is only open during the Summer season, or fly into Bozeman, Montana or Jackson Hole, Wyoming or Idaho Falls, Idaho. These are the closest airports to the Park. Your employer should provide you with information on getting from the airport to their offices.

◆◆◆

THE UNIFORM

The company you work for in the Park will provide you with a uniform. When Tracy got her acceptance letter to work for T.W. it described the uniform she would be required to wear. The letter described an unfashionable outfit. The letter was being complimentary. The uniforms are awful! Only the person who designed the uniform and that person's parents could like them.

The design of the uniforms are actually very functional, and after wearing them a couple of days and seeing all your friends in similar garb, no one notices. The uniforms are like what you wear off duty—no one cares; everyone is just glad to be in Yellowstone!

Only the Wranglers and Coach Drivers have somewhat decent duds. Polyester western shirt and furnish your own jeans.

You could wind up buying your outfit if you do not

The Clint Wilkes Original College Guide to a Summer Job in Yellowstone

Hannah from Alabama worked in the Gift Shop at Lake

Chris, a first year wrangler from Idaho State

turn it in at the end of your work agreement. They can deduct it from your last paycheck.

Different facilities within the Park open and close at

different times. The opening and closing dates will be in your application or you can call to get exact dates.

THE PAY

How much will you get paid? The answer always receives a look of disbelief. Remember, I mentioned you would not get rich working a Summer in Yellowstone. The pay varies by job. It is generally about $4.50 to $5.00 per hour. They take out about $8.50 per day for your meals in the E.D.R. and your housing. You will get exact details when you are offered a job.

If you have a complaint about the pay, write your Member of Congress. These companies are paying you what has been approved by Congress.

This is not a job where you will make a lot of money, unless you get a job as a Bell Porter or waiting tables. Then you will make a fortune in tips. (A very small fortune.)

A busser will be paid a percentage of the tips. A very unfortunate situation occured at one location where a couple of waiters were not giving the bussers their fair share of the tips. These two waiters were killed! No one has found where the bodies are hidden!

Upon further investigation, I discovered they were fired and went home.

If you get caught stealing from a fellow employee, then your employer will be the least of your worries.

In filling out your application, you will give the employer starting and ending dates you will be available to work. When you are offered a job, you will be given a "work agreement" with your dates of employment. If you leave your job prior to the end of your "work agreement" you will not be considered for rehire. However, you can give a two-week notice and quit.

Fill out the application with serious thought. These companies are counting on you to fulfill your committment. If a situation comes up where you must leave, try to talk with the Personnel Department if at all possible.

The most important part of your job to remember is, you are there to take care of the GUESTS. NEVER REFER TO A GUEST AS A TOURIST!!!!

When a Guest does something real stupid, they are referred to as "TOURONS". Do not get caught saying "TOURON".

For most of the GUESTS, this is a once in a lifetime experience. Whatever you do will make some kind of impact on the GUESTS.

After you have worked in the Park a couple of weeks, you most likely will consider yourself an expert on Yellowstone. You may even snicker to yourself when a guest asks a common question. Remember, the guest is experiencing Yellowstone for the first time. All of this is new for them. Also remember, when you first got to the Park, you probably went up to one of the seasoned veterans and asked them if you can see Old Faithful from Lake. (No, you cannot.)

The best example of talking with a guest was an observation I made of Old Faithful Inn employee Matt from Pittsburg. A guest asked Matt how to get to Morning Glory Pool. Matt could have said, "go out the front door, take a left and follow the signs." This is not what Matt did. He walked over to the front door with them, pointed out the start of the one mile walk. Then he told them they would pass Riverside and Grotto Geyser and since it was early in the season (mid May) to be on the lookout for Buffalo and Elk near the trail.

Having observed Matt during the Winter, I can attest he puts his heart into any conversation about Yellowstone.

I also heard of an employee who received a severe reprimand for not treating guests nicely. This employee cleaned cabins at the Old Faithful Lodge. Most of the cabins are within view of Old Faithful. When a guest would ask when to expect an eruption from Old Faithful, this employee would look at the steam of the geyser, look at their watch and say, "looks like in about thirty minutes."

It is impossible to tell from this kind of observation when Old Faithful will erupt. The approximate next eruption time is posted in many places in the Old Faithful area.

After several guests on tour busses told their tour guide about their conversation and how they had missed the eruption, this employee was reported. Many of the tour busses are only at Old Faithful for a couple of hours for lunch. This person could easily have been fired. This person did not intend to do wrong, but was not thinking. I cannot believe anyone would intentionally cause someone to miss an Old Faithful eruption.

Having told that story let me say this. Is it OK sometimes to have fun and "cut up" with the guests? The worst scenario is to tell your best joke and to have them look at you real odd, then to speak to one another in German or French.

Here is another reason it is not a good idea. There are people who cannot take a joke. Plus, always be aware of a spouse who may think you are flirting. Flirting! Yes, they will think you are flirting with their four hundred pound spouse!

The Clint Wilkes Original College Guide to a Summer Job In Yellowstone

If you still want to try a joke, have at it!

All of the people I have talked with who have ever been guests at Yellowstone have fond memories of their trip. It would be most unfortunate if you did something to steal that experience from them.

I know all of this sounds harsh, but T.W., Hamilton Stores and Y.P.S.S. are in the vacation business. They are doing the job of making people happy on their vacation. This is the reason they need you.

I heard of three employees who worked in the Park less than a week and were fired. They were out behind the Old Faithful Lodge which was not due to open for another few days. The Inn had opened the week prior.

During much of May, until the guests begin arriving in droves, buffalo will wander in close to the entire Old Faithful area. After Memorial Day, as the crowds increase, the buffalo will generally keep their distance from the buildings.

These three employees were throwing a frisbee at a buffalo!!! They had the great misfortune to be caught red-handed by a National Park Service Ranger.

These employers go to a lot of effort to make your summer one you will remember. They have an EMPLOYEE RECREATION DEPARTMENT to coordinate employee events. (Yes, you can apply for this job.) They offer a lot of employee discounts on the different activities in the Park. You will have your own lodging facilities away from the guests and your own Employee Dining Room,

(EDR). They even have a Pub for employees at most locations. Any person working in Yellowstone is allowed in the Pubs.

♦♦♦

You may have heard jobs become available during the summer. They do, but DO NOT go to Yellowstone in hopes of getting a job upon arrival. You could be the one in the "middle of nowhere" if you go to Yellowstone without any money and plan to get a job to pay your way home.

You could always call Yellowstone from home during the Summer to see if any openings have occurred. If they have jobs available, they will send you the paperwork and may hire you. Even if you got turned down on your initial application, you should still call and see if they will hire you at a later date.

If you want to check out Yellowstone before you ask for a job, you could do this: Plan a vacation to Yellowstone, complete with money to return home and money to be able to eat and sleep somewhere. Only under these conditions should you go to the Park without a "for sure" job.

In the Park you cannot sleep in your car. You must stay in a campground or lodging facility. You will get caught and you will get fined!

The people I have met LOVE working in Yellowstone. The type of people working there all seem to be having a great time.

Old Faithful

I would rather be in Yellowstone than anywhere in the world. I love the geysers of Yellowstone.

Old Faithful Geyser is the one sight everyone who visits Yellowstone wants to see. It was one of the first geysers to be named by the early explorers to Yellowstone.

The Old Faithful area contains over two-thirds of the world's geysers. To see most of the other geysers you would have to go to Iceland or New Zealand. I have asked a lot of people and no one knows where Iceland is. Plus, if you want to see geysers in an ice-land, then you should visit Yellowstone in the Winter. As far as New Zealand goes, why would anyone want to go to New Zealand when you could travel the same distance and see Australia. Quick! Name the capitol of New Zealand— see, no one knows anything about New Zealand.

Why is Old Faithful Geyser so faithful? It got its name precisely because it erupts on a somewhat regular, faithful schedule. There is a very scientific explanation which I will simplify. The availabilty of all of the water from snow and rain because of Yellowstone's location and elevation, plus the fact Yellowstone is in a caldera, (a caldera is a collapsed volcano). The heat and water gives you all the ingredients needed to have geysers. The natural plumbing system below Old Faithful works where water beneath Old Faithful heats up to a boiling point then erupts.

The length of the eruption taking place is directly related to the time until the next eruption. For example, if Old Faithful erupts for a short duration, then less water will need to be boiled for the next eruption. Vice versa then for a long eruption because it will take more time to recharge the water system.

The Rangers go out early each morning and use a stopwatch to time the length of the first eruption they observe. They then use a formula to determine, within several minutes, when the next eruption will occur. A Park Ranger will then time each eruption during the day and keep the next "eruption due time" posted at the Ranger Station visitor center and front desk of the three lodging facilities in the Old Faithful area. (Old Faithful Inn, Snow Lodge, Old Faithful Lodge). Scientists have determined the average time between eruptions is about seventy minutes. To see Old Faithful go from dormant steam to an exploding geyser, I strongly suggest arriving a few minutes before the "eruption due time".

You may have heard of some bizarre people who say the Army Corps of Engineers has installed pipes under Old Faithful to regulate the eruptions. These people probably hold an annual convention each year together with the people who have actually ridden in UFOs.

◆◆◆

The best experience in Yellowstone I have ever had was early one morning at Old Faithful. At home in Austin I get up about six every morning and go walking around Town Lake. I do most of my thinking when I am walking and try to walk where I do not need to pay a lot of attention. Since I am lost in thought I could easily get run over if I were near a busy street. This is one of the reasons I do not ride a bicycle. I am sure I would lose myself in thought and wind up under a truck. Besides that, have you ever seen someone on a mountain bike smiling? The ones I have seen were always pedaling with a look of near-death on their faces.

Anyway, I was staying at the Old Faithful Inn and was on one of these early morning walks. I was walking from the Inn toward the Lodge. As usual, I had my head down and I was deep in thought. I was on the walkway next to the benches which go by Old Faithful geyser. For some reason I looked up and was only a few feet from a gigantic set of Elk antlers. Behind the antlers were seven or eight of Mr Elk's wives. I froze instantly, only a few rows of benches were between me, Mr Elk and family. As startled as I was, it seemed apparent Mr. Elk could care less.

I started to slowly back away. Another guest was about twenty yards from me. He had a very expensive camera and motioned for me to "smile". Hesitating only briefly I smiled and he took my picture, with a herd of

Elk and Old Faithful beginning to erupt in the background. I walked slowly on over to him and gave him one of my business cards and asked him to please send me a copy of the picture. I was so excited I forgot to ask his name. I hoped I would see him later in the day so I could get his name and address to follow up on the picture. I never saw him.

I returned home and waited anxiously on the mail for several weeks. I finally gave up hope and forgot about the incident. Eight months later, I had an 8x10 envelope in the mail with a post mark from Ireland. It contained an incredible picture. There was no return address and no note in the envelope. When this book reaches world wide circulation, I hope he reads this so I can say, "thank you, kind stranger".

Let me make this very clear. Never approach any animal, it will most likely be bad for the animal or you. The reason I was so scared was the Elk could have

Elk near a residence at Mammoth are a common sight.

attacked me with those antlers at any time. In retrospect, I should not have even stopped briefly to have my picture taken.

If you stumble upon an animal like I did, remain calm and back out of the situation. Read all of the Ranger brochures about what to do if you encounter a bear or any animal. The safest thing to do when you are on a hike or in the wilderness is to make noise. The animals will normally do their part to avoid you. (Always take your bells and a whistle with you.)

The Geyser areas have many Park Service provided walkways. If you were to get off the walkways, there are many areas you could be severely or mortally injured. Bicycles are not allowed on the wooden walkways for the bicyclist's safety. If they accidentally rode off the walkway, they could land in a scalding pool of water. I have seen young kids riding their bikes on the walkways—with their parents !!

The Old Faithful area has three hotels and a lot of cabins.
The summer season begins first in Yellowstone at Old Faithful. The Old Faithful Inn is the first lodging facility to open inside the Park. It will open about the first weekend in May, followed by the Snow Lodge and the Old Faithful Lodge during the next two weeks.

The most famous Inn in the world is here, The Old Faithful Inn. This building is truly magnificent. The Lobby alone is worth visiting. It contains a huge fireplace which is many times burning on the cool summer mornings and evenings. Off the lobby are both a large restaurant and a bar. An Ice Cream shop and fast food place are down the hall.

The restaurant at the Old Faithful Inn serves a magnificent breakfast buffet. They also serve lunch. For dinner you need reservations to be assured of a table. You can wait in line for dinner.

This summer I arrived in Gardiner, Montana in early May, the day before the Old Faithful Inn was scheduled to open. The next day I headed for Old Faithful. I waited till mid-afternoon to drive the fifty miles to the Inn and start meeting employees.

The first employee I met had an employee name tag saying her name was Rebecca and her home state was Alabama. She had graduated from high school only a few days prior to arriving in Yellowstone. Both her Aunt and a family friend had worked in the Park years ago. Rebecca had been planning this summer for as long as she could remember.

Each time I talked with her she would tell me of a different hike or Yellowstone adventure.

The one item she made sure was top quality was her hiking boots. Her dad had gotten her a lot of equipment to go on hikes. She and her dad both made sure she had the best boots.

My third week in Yellowstone I caught a twenty-four hour flu bug. I was in my tent about midnight as the bug started. I got up, threw all my camping equipment in my car and checked into a hotel. The next day was awful! One of those sick feelings you hate to have. It left that evening almost as quickly as it came. I was going to live!

A week later I was walking through the side entrance of the Old Faithful Inn, headed for the breakfast buffet. I am an early riser, it was about 7 A.M. As I walked down the hall I approached the side entrance to the gift shop. I did not have my glasses, and these halls near the lobby are dimly lit. I was sure I could see Rebecca standing in the hall. She was dressed in a sweat shirt and sweat pants. As I got closer I recognized the look on her face. Rebecca had the flu bug! I knew exactly how she felt. She had my sympathy!

She saw me and said, "hello Clint". She tried to smile but she and I both knew that was impossible.

I asked if she was O.K. She replied she was waiting on the manager to ask for the day off. I asked her why she had not just called on the phone. She said, in a weak voice, " I know she would believe me if I called, but I want to be sure she knows I really am sick."

I told Rebecca I hoped she would feel better soon and I headed to the restaurant. A few days later I was talking to my sister on the phone. I was telling Sis how impressed I was with Rebecca getting out of her sick bed to go tell her boss she could not work that day.

My sister listened to my story, then asked me, "didn't you tell me the dorms are about a fifteen minute walk behind the Old Faithful Inn?" I replied, "yes". I did not have a clue why Sis would ask this. Then she asked a question which even now causes me terrible embarassment. Sis asked, " did you offer to give her a ride back to her dorm?"

Not only did I not ask, I never even thought of it! The worst part is, I know how bad she felt. I had suffered this only a week prior!

The Clint Wilkes Original College Guide to a Summer Job in Yellowstone

I have not said anything to Rebecca. I now offer my apology. I do hope she had gotten a friend to drive her back to her dorm that morning.

I saw her several times over the next few weeks. Her recovery was complete.

Being a responsible employee for T.W. or any other company has its rewards.

I had been working different parts of the Park plus making trips to Jackson Hole and other towns during June. I had not seen Rebecca in a couple of weeks.

Wednesday night is Park employees night at *Eino's*. Wednesday is also payday, so *Eino's* is always packed with Park employees. I try to get to *Eino's* to talk with people on most Wednesdays.

I did my standard introduction, telling how I am writing a book after introducing myself to one young lady. She turned toward her friend standing nearby and said, "Hanna, this is the man Rebecca told us about." Hanna came over and the three of us introduced ourselves. I was talking to Rebecca's two best friends, Ashley and Hanna. They had also just graduated from Daphne High School and planned to attend Faulkner College in the Fall.

They told me they worked at Lake Lodge. Ashley is a cashier in the cafeteria and Hanna works in the gift shop.

As we talked I was trying to figure out why Rebecca had not told me about her two friends working at Lake.

I soon solved the mystery. I asked how long they had been in Yellowstone. Ashley replied, "Rebecca called us about a week ago and told us to get to Yellowstone quick, this place is fantastic!" They had called T.W. and given Rebecca as a reference. T.W. called them back a few hours later and offered them jobs. The next day they were on flights to Bozeman and were at work the following day.

I looked forward to seeing Rebecca and telling her I had met her friends.

Getting a job this way is unusual, but it does happen. I would bet the farm they got hired because Rebecca is such a responsible employee. Obviously T.W. had called Rebecca's boss to find out what kind of employee she was. T.W. and every other employer in the world wants responsible workers. In most cases responsible employees will have responsible friends.

I talked with all of these ladies during the summer. T.W. was the big winner with these three employees!

◆◆◆

I met several other employees that opening day at the Old Faithful Inn. One of these was also from Alabama. Chantal will be a junior at Auburn this Fall. She saw an ad in the Auburn placement office telling of summer jobs in Yellowstone. She had no idea what working in Yellowstone would be like. This did not cause her to hesitate one moment in filling out the application.

After briefly talking with her it was obvious she would be very successful in the career she was majoring in. Her manner and enthusiasim are a perfect combination for a future journalist. Within minutes of our first meeting it was Chantal asking me questions about writing this book.

On subsequent conversations, I discovered more about her and her adventurous spirit. She had spent last summer working as a Nanny on Cape Cod. This also was a job she knew nothing about until she had seen an ad in the Auburn placement office.

Chantal did know one thing about working in Yellowstone. She had applied for a job working in the gift shop, and had put on her application she could start work as soon as the Old Faithful Inn opened. She went on to write she would be willing to take off the Spring quarter at Auburn if she were offered a job in the Gift Shop. Her friend, Sharon from Auburn, did not arrive till the Spring quarter ended. She worked in Housekeeping.

Over the course of the summer Chantal and I became friends. On many occasions I would meet her and her friend Daniel for lunch in the E.D.R.

I never knew when Chantal would have her thirty minute meal break. I would have to go by the gift shop and just hope it was near time for her break. On one occasion I went by late one afternoon. It was a rainy and, even though it was mid-July, snowy day. This meant all the tourists were inside the Old Faithful Inn. Most of those were shopping at the gift shop. Chantal was working the register. The check-out line to pay was the longest I had ever seen.

Another TW employee was standing with Chantel behind the register doing nothing. Chantal was looking at the price on each item, ringing it up, taking the payment and putting the merchandise in a bag. She had a most harried look. Hers was not a smiling face.

I stood where she could see me if she ever looked up. I began to wonder if that was ever going to happen!

After several minutes she saw me and a huge smile came over her face. The first thing she said was, "I go on break in ten minutes, meet me at the front door."

I met her and we headed for the Old Faithful Inn E.D.R. It is located below the main lobby. You go down a set of stairs and past the dungeon to reach the E.D.R.

Chantal began to tell me about the guy she was

working with. She asked if I had noticed him. I told her I had observed him doing nothing.

She said he had worked in the gift shop for several weeks and still was clueless as to how to check out a customer. He was supposed to be helping by telling her the price of the items, then she would ring it up, take the payment and he would bag the item. He was incapable of understanding this concept.

With customers becoming impatient, Chantal turned to him and whispered in her most polite and southern voice. "Please get out of the way, I can do this faster without you."

This may not be **exactly** what she said, but it was something to that effect.

Chantal then looked at me and said, "Clint, guess what he did?" I told Chantal I could not imagine what he would have done. Her answer surprised me. Chantal said, "he told on me!"

I told my god-daughter April this story and asked her what she thought. April said, "the last time I heard of someone telling on someone, I was twelve years old!"

Chantal did not get in trouble, but the manager did tell her to try to be more patient with this person.

When I first met Chantal she had one of the best haircuts I had ever seen on a young woman. In this day of political correctness, I did not pay her a compliment on her hair style.

One day late in the summer, I was with Daniel in the Hamilton Store next to the Snow Lodge waiting to meet Chantal. We were going to *Eino's* for dinner.

As Chantal approached, I was aghast! She had gotten a haircut! I said nothing!

The best way to describe the haircut was a comment made by one of Chantal's friends when we entered

Eino's. As we walked in the friend walked up, looked at Chantal's haircut, and said, "whatever possessed you to cut your hair?"

You probably think I am some kind of big jerk for writing this story. I'm not. I ran this story by Chantal and asked her if it was O.K. to write it. She thought it was hilarious and said O.K.

I have met several college students from my home state of Alabama and my adopted state of Texas working at the Inn. Kathryn from Alabama works as a STORE-KEEPER, helping keep up with all the inventory needed to keep the Old Faithful Inn open.

When you apply for a job, it is important for you to let T.W. and the other companies know what you can do for them. Your circumstances may not allow you to take off a quarter from school, but there are other things you can do. You can give excellent references. They do check to see if they are true! You can also describe responsibilities you have had on previous jobs.

Another Old Faithful employee with a unique background was Lee from Utah. Lee had worked at the Grand Canyon, another T.W. run concession, last summer. He told me about the Grand Canyon experience which I did find interesting, but to me not nearly as interesting as working at Yellowstone.

The unique story came up several weeks after first

meeting Lee. In an off hand comment he mentioned how he was fast with a six-gun. Not being able to ask a tactful question, I looked at Lee and said, "what are you talking about?" Lee went on to tell me how several years ago he had been the "bad guy" (in a black hat) in a wild west shootout held on a dude ranch in Arizona. Three times a day during the week, with an extra show on weekends, he would shoot the deputy in the back before coming to an untimely demise at the hands of a faster gun worn by the Sheriff (in the white hat).

As Lee described this, it sounded like it was a lot of fun. (Though not as good as working at Yellowstone.)

When my summer at Yellowstone ended, I checked to see if Lee's Yellowstone roommate had fared any better than his former Arizona roommate. All was fine, this roommate had not been shot once in the back. I did find out Lee had hit him with a pillow a couple of times for snoring!

The job of Bell Porter at Old Faithful is one of the best and hardest jobs to get in Yellowstone. It is one of the best because you make a lot of money in tips. It is one of the hardest to get because no one ever quits. The Bell Porters I talked with all seemed to say this was their seventh or tenth or whatever year to work a Summer in Yellowstone. Many of them also work in the Winter.

Charlotte is the manager of the Bell Porters at the Inn. She is the Bell Captain. This is her twelfth summer working in Yellowstone. She was very busy the first time I saw her.

Opening day of the Old Faithful Inn is controlled

chaos.

Later I would see many other women Bell Porters, but during this afternoon Charlotte was the only woman.

I wanted to talk to her, but I try not to interfere with employees at work. As I infrequently observed her during that day, I saw her picking up trash a thoughtless guest had left in the parking area. Later I saw her helping a couple whose seven year old son had briefly disappeared.

I was anxious to talk with her, but the opportunity never arose. That night I had a horrible dream. I almost never have bad dreams but this one was a doozey!

In this dream I finally had an opportunity to talk with Charlotte and stuck my foot firmly in my mouth. I never, ever, ever refer to women over the age of thirteen as girls. I will call them young ladies and I always call women over eighteen women.

I picked what was probably one of the worst possible moments to approach Charlotte. Timing is important in dreams! She had been up to her ears in luggage for several hours and had finally gotten a breather. She was resting in a corner taking what was possibly her first drink of water for the dream day. Imagine you are Charlotte and some man you have never seen before walks up and says, " are you the only girl working here today?" Someone had made an incredibly dumb statement. I recognized the voice and knew it was mine. I cannot believe I did not wake up then! I have no idea who was more stunned, Charlotte or me. How could I say something so incredibly stupid even in a dream! This has never been my attitude toward women. When I am awake I have even corrected other men, in an all men group, when they have referred to one of my colleagues or friends as a girl.

Charlotte knew, as an employee of T.W., she could not call me a moron, even though it was only a dream. What she did say was polite, but she had a "you are a moron" look on her face. I stuttered and tried to start over. I apologized for the way I had asked the question. Now I am sure I looked like a moron apologizing. She was most gracious to answer a few questions and I left feeling about as bad as I have ever felt. As I walked off, the alarm clock rang.

I talked to Charlotte a few days later and she was very nice. I would not want to think what might have really happened if I had called this hard working woman and manager of the other Porters a girl. In reality I would probably have had a stroke!

I rarely say something really dumb. I have met Presidents Ford, Carter, Reagan, Bush and Clinton, (and future president Bob Kerrey). On these brief encounters, I have always made a coherent remark. I even spoke briefly with Mrs Carter shortly before the election of 1980. President Carter was about as low as you could get in the polls. As I walked through the receiving line I could see the people before me were not being rude, but were also not saying anything very encouraging. When my turn came to shake her hand, I looked at her and said, "Mrs Carter, your husband has my confidence." The First Lady looked at me and smiled. I am sure she does not remember all the thousands of people she has met, but I am proud to know I brought one brief smile to her face that day.

The last time I remember saying something really

dumb was when I met David Gergen. Mr Gergen had been a key player in the Reagan White House and has also been a top advisor to President Clinton.

I was changing planes several years ago at DFW. I was walking down the skyway and saw Mr. Gergen approaching. He had been out of the Reagan administration for a couple of years and was a frequent guest on political talk shows. Most people did not recognize him, but I did. I love those shows!

When I first saw Mr Gergen he was only a few steps away. I looked at him and said, " excuse me, aren't you David Gergen?" He replied he was indeed David Gergen, as he kept walking. I then made my dumb comment. I said, "I have met President Reagan." He gave me a curious look, said, "that's nice", and proceeded past me on his way.

◆◆◆

The Old Faithful Inn is nearly one hundred years old. Any building this old would have to have rumors of ghosts. Yellowstone is no exception.

Kristi and Adam were two of my favorite people at Yellowstone. Adam is from New York and had moved to Mississippi to go to college and live with his Aunt. Kristi was one of the top high school tennis players in Mississippi and was on a tennis scholarship to Birmingham Southern College in Alabama.

After spending her entire life in competitive tennis, Kristi decided to take a year off from both school and tennis. She and Adam will work in Yellowstone, then hope to work at the Grand Canyon during the Winter. Then back to Yellowstone next summer before returning to school and the court.

Adam will most likely wind up in court also, as a lawyer! Adam would make a terrific lawyer. His mind is always searching for answers. He is most interesting to talk with.

The conversations with Kristi and Adam could always go in any direction. On one occasion as we talked Adam said, "Kristi, tell Clint about last Monday night at the Inn." Kristi told an eerie story of how she, Adam and several friends were having a conversation late one night on the Observation deck of the Old Faithful Inn. It was past midnight. She left the group to go to the ladies' room. The hallways closest to the lobby area are dimly lit. She walked down the hall and entered the restroom. As she was leaving she tried to open the stall door. She could see the lock was definitely not locked, but the door would not open! She pulled on the door again and it opened. Then she turned to go toward the exit door leading to the hallway. She could not see the door; the wall was solid without a door. A sense of being scared permeated her body. She blinked and rubbed her eyes. As she opened them, she saw the door. She rejoined Adam and her buddies, but decided against telling them of her adventure.

An hour later, Adam left the group to go to the men's room. Kristi knew Adam was really going to smoke a cigarette. He had promised to quit and had cut back a lot.

The men's room has a ledge to sit on with windows you can open. Adam was sitting there when he heard one of the stall doors slam shut. He knew no one had entered since he could see the entrance door. Even though there was no wind, he assumed it still must have been the wind which caused the door to slam. He also decided to only smoke half his cigarette.

Then the lights went out! They were only out a couple of seconds and Adam was already headed to the door when they came on. He had taken three steps when he noticed there were windows in **front** of him. That was impossible! He had just gotten up from sitting next to the windows, plus he had taken three steps. He turned **behind** him and **there** was the door! Adam did not hesitate to think how could this be possible. He got out of there!

Adam also did not tell the group about his encounter.

The next day he could not hold off telling Kristi. They exchanged stories.

Do I believe in ghosts? Maybe. Do I believe Kristi and Adam? Yes!

◆◆◆

OLD FAITHFUL LODGE

Across from Old Faithful Geyser is the Old Faithful Lodge with its cabins. The Lodge is a more modern structure with a cafeteria, gift shop, ice cream shop and muffin/cookie shop.

You go into the Lodge to rent the cabins. The cabins are a short walk behind the Lodge. You can park close to your cabin. The cabins are available with or without bath. The showers are located inside the Lodge, in the back hallway.

The cafeteria offers a wide variety of food. They serve Pizza till 4:00pm. At 4:00 they keep all the other offerings, take down the Pizza area and replace it with a nightly dinner special. The cafeteria is excellent, almost as good as Frank's T.E.C. cafeteria in Austin.

The ice cream shop and muffin/cookie shop are

under the same direction. The employees will alternate working in these two shops in the Lodge. The hours of operation are from early morning till mid evening. You will work all shifts.

T.W. also operates the gift shops which are in the lobbies of all the lodging facilities. The Lodge gift shop is one of the largest. It has a fudge shop in addition to all the t-shirts and other gifts . The fudge is made each day in the shop. Forget your diet if you work here.

In the back of the gift shop is an operating pottery shop. The potter has worked in Yellowstone each summer for the past twelve years.

An excellent artist is in the lobby of the Lodge. His work is incredible.

◆◆◆

SNOW LODGE

Several hundred yards from the famous geyser is the Snow Lodge. It is more of a dorm type building, with separate women's and men's restrooms and shower facilities for the rooms which do not have bathrooms. I have stayed here several times and was pleased. The Snow Lodge has a restaurant for breakfast, lunch and dinner. This restaurant does not require dinner reservations.

Many cabins are located behind the Snow Lodge.

◆◆◆

The Four Seasons Deli and ice cream shop is within close walking distance to the Geyser. The hungrier you are, the better the food tastes. The ice cream is always good!

◆◆◆

Observation Point is about a thirty minute walk up a hill from behind Old Faithful. I have been there for both day and night eruptions. I suggest you do either and preferably both. A night with a full moon creates an extraordinary scene. Along with your whistle, you will need a good flashlight for a nighttime excursion.

A United States Post Office is open during the Summer at Old Faithful. It is next to the Snow Lodge.

Buffalo and Elk are a common sight around Old Faithful. They can wander very close to the buildings. Please be careful. If Buffalo are on one of the trails it is very smart to NOT go near them. These animals may look like they would be slow but a buffalo could outrun an NFL wide receiver in a fifty yard dash.

Buffalo do not like or want to be petted!

There are two Hamilton Stores and a Hamilton Photo Shop at Old Faithful. The Hamilton Store next to the Inn has a grocery store, gift shop and short order restaurant in it. Breakfast at this Hamilton Store is great.

The other Hamilton Store next to the Snow Lodge is also a complete store except it has microwave sandwiches. It does not have a short order grill. If you are on vacation and hate to cook then you will like the food.

The Hamilton Photo Shop offers one hour film developing with a limited supply of gifts and snacks.

The Old Faithful area is always hectic. Probably 99% of all visitors to Yellowstone will spend time at Old Faithful. Compare this to some other areas which may only see half or more of the guests. The employees I have talked with who work at Old Faithful all seem to enjoy it. They realize if the crowds start to get to them, all they have to do is walk a couple of hundred yards and they are in the wilderness. (I hope with their whistle.) Some of the veterans of many seasons at Old Faithful have built a Frisbee Golf Course in an area isolated, but still close to the Inn.

The employees I talked with who do not work at Old Faithful will hardly ever go to the famous geyser area. They do not want to get into the traffic and crowds. Tracy did not go to Old Faithful at all her first Summer, and I had to pay her to go her second Summer. Once you see Roosevelt you will understand why.

It seems like every employee I talked with was convinced the area they worked was the best. Having seen all the Park I can understand why.

The Clint Wilkes Original College Guide to a Summer Job in Yellowstone

Emily, a wrangler, going on a stagecoach ride on her off day.

Roosevelt

Roosevelt is my favorite place to stay in the Park. I enjoy all of the other areas, but I especially like the rustic appeal of the cabins. Only the Lobby of the Old Faithful Inn can compare to Roosevelt Lodge for rustic charm.

The best meal in the Park is served on the Roosevelt Cookout at Yancy's Hole late each afternoon. Be sure to make reservations in advance if you have friends coming to visit you in the Park.

There are two ways to get to the cookout. You can ride in one of the wagons which takes about thirty minutes to get to Yancy's Hole. You can also take one of the the horseback ride tours. There are two versions, either a one hour ride or two hour ride out to Yancy's Hole. Both return in about a twenty minute ride directly to the corrals at Roosevelt after dinner. I have taken both and would recommend either.

Be sure to remember your horse's name.

After dinner, you will need to tell the Wranglers your horse's name in order for them to retrieve it from the holding area. On my first trip I was given a horse named *Riprock*. I thought this was a dumb name for a horse so I renamed him *Texas Tornado*, and then I forgot his original name. He looked very unhappy with the name *Riprock* and I could tell immediatly how happy he was with the new name, *Texas Tornado*.

Unfortunatly, after dinner when I told Josh from Arizona, one of the Wranglers, my horse's name was *Texas Tornado*, he did not have a clue which horse I was talking about. I had to wait til all the horses were assigned to get *Texas Tornado*. It was worth it because I had the best of all the horses. I understand the Wranglers let him keep his new name.

I mentioned this was the best meal in the Park. It is! Steaks are cooked over an open fire, the corn is delicious along with the cole slaw and corn muffins. Roosevelt has an exclusive on the way they cook beans for the cookout. They combine several different beans cooked in a special way. I am a terrible cook so I have never thought to ask for the Roosevelt Beans recipe. They also have a delicious cobbler each night.

Most likely you have never had "Cowboy Coffee" before. I am not a coffee drinker, but I did notice everyone going back for refills.

An adventure can happen at any time in Yellowstone. Tracy worked in Activities at Roosevelt both of her summers in the Park. At the end of the second summer, a group of guests were on their way to Yancy's Hole for the cookout. The Cooks always arrive early on the chuckwagon. They start the fire and prepare the steaks so they can begin grilling shortly after all the guests arrive.

The wagons and both horseback ride tours are timed to arrive close to the same time. One horseback group had arrived and was tieing up. The wagons were about two hundred yards from their destination. The second horseback group was not yet in sight of Yancy's Hole. Everything appeared to the Wranglers the way it had every day that summer.

Erica from Washington State, one of the Wranglers, was the first to see the new guests. The newest guests were soon to give over two hundred and fifty other guests the thrill of their vacation. The uninvited guests caught Erica's attention as they lumbered slowly out of the woods west of the camp sight.

You would expect two giant Grizzly Bears, weighing over one thousand combined pounds, to be in a hurry to get to the gourmet feast which awaited them. It was obvious they knew who was in charge. It was not Erica and company.

The Cooks made a brilliant move and headed East to the wagons. Let me rephrase that. They QUICKLY headed East toward the wagons! The Wranglers gathered all the guests in what should be a safe place behind the wagons. They could not leave because the Grizzlys could easily startle the horses.

The Grizzlys proceeded to do what they do best. They ate every smidgen of food in the camp. It was an incredible sight.

The Park Rangers arrived and took control. They are trained in confrontations with Bears. Using sleeping darts, they shot the bears. They later had the Grizzlys transported many miles from Roosevelt in hopes they would not return to Yancy's Hole.

Sadly, if they were to return, the Park Service might have to destroy them. Any time you encounter a wild animal and feed it or in some way treat it like a pet, you are doing it a great disservice. These animals must survive all year in the wilderness. Feeding an animal lessons its ability to gather its own food. Any time the Park Service must intervene between a guest and an animal, it is the animal who becomes the big loser.

The end of this story is most surprising. Not a single guest asked for a refund for the meal they did not get to eat.

◆◆◆

Roosevelt has several cabins which have complete bathrooms and electric heat. I have only stayed in one of these once. I prefer the "Rustic Shelter" cabins. These have no bath or water and the heat is a wood burning stove. They furnish one or two compressed saw dust fire logs and a wax lighter. After the first morning I learned the "trick" of getting my logs lit. (Start with a small chunk of log, do not try to light it all at once.) The showers are a convenient walk from the cabins. The walk can be chilly early in the morning, but the showers are heated and comfortable.

The Roosevelt Lodge Restaurant is excellent. Bob Barbee, the past Superintendent of Yellowstone, was a frequent guest. I have talked with many waitstaff, who all say Mr. Barbee was a good guy. (He should be, he had the best job in the world. Now he is the Director of the Park Service in Alaska.)

It is about thirty miles from Roosevelt to Cooke City. Most nights a lot of Roosevelt employees will go to Cooke City. It has several very good restaurants and other things to do.

K-Bar in Gardiner is a favorite destination for many Roosevelt employees.

Sean was the Head Wrangler at Roosevelt this sum-

Sean, Roosevelt Head Wrangler

mer. Sean is from New Mexico and gives every appearance of being the perfect "cowboy". He has been at Roosevelt three years, the previous two as a Wrangler. Before coming to Yellowstone he had been foreman of a large cattle ranch in New Mexico. Sean had gotten a call from a friend asking if he was interested in working as a Wrangler in the Park. Sean was very happy in New Mexico and told his friend this. Less than a month later the owner of the ranch died. Sean called to see if a Wrangler position was still open.

It was very interesting talking with Sean. He is a wealth of knowledge about the Park, horses and being a Wrangler. After about an hour of talking, I asked him a question I was sure I knew the answer to. I asked him when he got his first horse. I already knew the answer would be something like, when he was three. Sean answered differently. He had not been interested in horses til he was a senior in high school. During his high school senior year he got a part time job and saved up for his first horse.

After he left New Mexico State he was offered a job working on a cattle ranch. He has been a "cowboy" ever since.

I met Greg the day Roosevelt opened. His name tag

Greg from Jacksonville State University in Alabama

told me he was Greg from Alabama. The first opportunity I had I introduced myself. I asked him where he was from, he replied, "Anniston". When I told him I went to Jacksonville State, he grinned and said he was a Senior at Jacksonville State. Greg was a great help to me all summer.

Greg has worked at Roosevelt three summers. This

summer he is Lead Wrangler. He and Sean are a terrific team.

Emily worked as a Hostess and in the E.D.R. and as a Wrangler.

Emily will be a junior next year at the University of Vermont. She is studying to be a Vet. She has been to equestrian camp every summer for the past five years. She is an accomplished rider in both Western and the more difficult English riding styles.

Emily wanted to be a Wrangler in Yellowstone. She filled out a T.W. application and put her first job choice was to be a Wrangler. She also put on her application she would take any job available.

Emily got hired to work at Roosevelt......in the E.D.R. Her job was to serve meals and help prepare the food. She was an excellent worker.

At least once a day after she arrived, Emily would talk to Sean, the Head Wrangler, about becoming a Wrangler. Early in the season Sean did not have a

Wrangler position available.

Lady Luck smiled on Emily two and a half weeks after arriving. The Wranglers were hired to arrive on a staggered schedule. One of those scheduled to arrive called to say he would not be coming.

Just like she had done every day since arriving, Emily went to the corrals to visit Sean and to see the horses. On this day Emily was told to saddle up *Jake* and go for a ride and interview with Greg, Catherine and John.

Emily was offered the job before they were out of sight of the corrals.

A Black Bear near Roosevelt

Roosevelt does not open till the second week in June. The Park Service wants to make sure all the bears are awake and have eaten plenty of carcass, roots and berries. Roosevelt is "BEAR COUNTRY".

The only time you want to see a bear in Yellowstone is when you are in your car and the bear is in a field several hundred yards away.

The next story may or may not be true.

Several years ago, the government spent several million of our tax dollars to distinguish the difference between Black Bear scat and Grizzly scat in Yellowstone. In appearance they are identical. After several months with the leading bear scientists in the world working on the study, they came to this conclusion: The Grizzly scat contains the most bells and whistles.

I do not think this story is true. I never actually read about the scat study. Then I got to thinking maybe the story is true. This is the same government that spent several hundred thousand dollars to study flatulence of cows. If you are not laughing, you do not know that flatulence is the scientific word for "farting".

I was at Roosevelt the afternoon it opened.

I met Jack and his wife, Ruth, two of the most charming people I have ever met. They have worked for Hamilton Stores for many years and have managed the Roosevelt store the past four years.

Jack was kind enough to show me their apartment located close to the store. They have a great collection of early 1900 Old Faithful photographs.

Roosevelt was the location for one of the best "love stories" I heard about. I was fortunate to be able to meet both of these people.

The Clint Wilkes Original College Guide to a Summer Job in Yellowstone

"Sheriff" Shawn and Miss Marian, "the Pretty School Marm"

If this story had taken place in the Old West, it would have gone like this:

Shawn was the John Wayne type sheriff and number one cowboy in town. He was often referred to as "Shawn Wayne".

Shawn delt justice fairly and was well respected. The town's children and old folks knew Shawn would keep the peace. The ladies knew Shawn would be a wonderful husband, but they also knew the law was his true love.

Everything changed for Shawn the day Miss Marian, the pretty school marm, arrived in town. Shawn was in love!

Shawn was a brave and courageous sheriff. He was also very shy. He could not get the nerve to ask Miss Marian, the pretty school marm, for a date.

The terrible Touron Gang was on the rampage

across the west. They heard about Miss Marian, the pretty school marm, who had been in town for the past six months. She had raised the schools S.A.T. scores over thirty percent.

The Touron Gang consisted of Mom and Dad Touron and Kid Touron. He was called Kid because he was ten years old. His real name was Billy, but "Billy the Kid" was already taken.

The Touron Gang ravaged the west in their oversized covered wagon pulled by two giant mules named Winnie and Baygo. Behind the giant wagon they pulled a smaller, compact sized buckboard wagon. You could hear Mom and Dad yelling, "go Winnie, go Baygo". Sometimes they would yell the names together, "go WinnieBaygo".

The evil Touron Gang kidnapped Miss Marian, the pretty school marm, and sent a ransom note to Sheriff Shawn.

Shawn Wayne read the note aloud. "We have kidnapped Miss Marian, the pretty school marm, and demand to eat dinner at the Lake Hotel *without* making reservations!"

Shawn knew this demand was impossible. NOBODY, gets to eat at Lake *without* reservations!

Shawn put out the call for a possee to rescue Miss Marian, the pretty school marm. He planned to ask Miss Marian, the pretty school marm, to marry him.

The first member of the posse Shawn recruited was his sidekick Sean. The two of them together sometimes created confusion because their names are pronounced the same. Someone would yell, "look out Shawn", referring to the Sheriff and Sean would hit the deck thinking they were calling for him to look out.

The next recruit was Sean's sidekick Greg. Greg then

called on his sidekick Jess, who called on his sidekick Ron, who called on his sidekick Earl. This went on until they reached Mike, the last cowboy in town. Mike did not have a sidekick and looked forward to a new cowboy coming to town so he would have a sidekick. He did have Blackie who looked just like that Lab on the Black Dog Ale bottle.

The posse took off after the Touron Gang and Miss Marian, the pretty school marm.

The chase was terrible. The posse got behind the wagon and if it gave a right turn signal it would turn left. Sometimes it would turn without any turn signal. Sometimes the big wagon would stop in the middle of the road instead of using the pullouts provided for stopping. The chase indeed was terrible!

Miss Marian, the pretty school marm, was finally saved because of a bear.

The Touron Gang's wagon topped a hill and there off two hundred yards from the road, was a large grizzly. The Tourons stopped in the middle of the road as Dad Touron grabbed his video recorder and headed for the bear. Every member of the posse passed Dad Touron with their own video cameras. All wanted to photograph the grizzly.

All except for Shawn Wayne! He climbed into the back of the wagon silently as Mom Touron and the Kid watched Dad video record the bear.

Sheriff Shawn untied the rope holding Miss Marian, the pretty school marm. As the last bit of rope was untied Miss Marian, the pretty school marm looked at Sheriff Shawn and said, "I love you."

They headed back to Sheriff Shawn's horse while giving one another a passionate kiss.

They were married three months later.

Shawn would continue to uphold justice, but he would have his bride at his side to help him.

This is not the Old West, this is the New West. Here is what really happened:

Marian first met Shawn when they both were working as Wranglers at Roosevelt. Marian had been working over a month when Shawn arrived.

Dating was something neither thought about. These two Wranglers were typical of all of the people working at Roosevelt. They were best friends.

They worked together the entire summer and even though there were no thoughts of love, by the end of the summer, they were best of friends. The best way to describe them would be "sidekicks".

Marian left Yellowstone to return to Kentucky. She and Shawn did not see each other for three years.

Shawn was promoted to Head Wrangler while Marian was away. Marian returned and was promoted to Lead Wrangler, a position she earned because of her numerous credentials and qualifications with horses.

This summer would be different for Shawn and Marian. If Shawn had asked Marian for a date three years earlier she probably would have said no. This summer Marian hoped Shawn would ask her out.

Shawn asked Marian for a date and they were married eighteen months later.

If you ask either one who they married, the reply will be, "I am lucky enough to be in love and married to my best friend."

Shawn was one of the most popular Head Wranglers to ever work in Yellowstone. His last summer as Head Wrangler almost 90% of the previous summers Wranglers returned to once again work for Shawn. Usually 40% would be a high return rate for any job.

Marian and Shawn are now living in Gardiner.

A modern day "Touron Gang"

Two great jobs are at Roosevelt. Tommy from Auburn has had one of them for the past two summers. The gift shop in Roosevelt Lodge is teeney-tiny. Most people, like me, think it is part of the front desk. It is not, it is a seperate department.

I met Tommy when Mammoth Hotel opened. He worked there for a couple of weeks until Roosevelt opened. Tommy was very popular with his bosses and co-workers. They all wanted him to stay at Mammoth. Tommy would just smile and tell them he was off to Roosevelt as soon as it opened.

I had seen Chantel, also from Auburn, several times at the Old Faithful Inn gift shop as she would return from the "dungeon". Her responsibility was keeping the t-shirt bins full. The T-shirts are kept in the basement. Because it is hot, dusty and just plain unpleasant, it is referred to as the "dungeon". As Chantel would return to the air conditioned gift shop it was obvious she had been working hard.

On the other hand Tommy probably spends only a few minutes restocking the entire gift shop at Roosevelt.

I have never heard either Chantel or anyone working in the gift shops complain about their jobs. They all have friends in housekeeping and know better than to complain.

Tommy is smiling for two reasons - one, this photo shows the entire gift shop. Two, he just got accepted to law school. Congratulations, Tommy!!!

The only "complaint" Chantel, Tommy, and other Auburn students have is the same "complaint" Aggies, Oklahoma State, and Florida State students have. Some Crimson Tide fan will go up to Tommy or Chantel and see their name tag with Chantel from Alabama on it. This fan will then say "Roll Tide", expecting an echo. All employees are polite to guests, Tommy and Chantel are no exception. They will nicely tell the guest they go to Auburn. I would bet they say "War Eagle" silently as the guests walk away.

The other great job at Roosevelt is in Activity Sales. The Activity Sales office is located in front of the corrals. Wranglers from Canyon and Mammoth are great, but still it sure looked to me like the Wranglers from Roosevelt were working the hardest and having the most fun!

The Roosevelt Activity Sales office always has Wranglers around it.

Lake Yellowstone

The Lake Yellowstone area is referred to as LAKE. If you enjoy being on the water, Lake is the place for you. Lake is great for boating and fishing, but be prepared for some cold water if you decide to jump in. If you want to go swimming, bring a wetsuit.

To give you an example of how cold the water is, try this: Take a bucket of ice cubes and put them in the crisper part of your refrigerator (that's where you keep the lettuce). The instant the ice cubes have changed from solid to liquid is about the temperature the water in Lake stays all summer.

In the Summer, if you are near Lake during a storm,

you should be able to see the rainbows which will form over the Lake once the storm ends.

Lake Hotel opens in mid May. The opening of Lake is as different as night and day from the Old Faithful Inn opening of the week before.

The Lake Hotel is not overrun with guests on the day it opens. Only the Hotel and the cabins are ready for visitors. The Lodge, located a short distance away, will not open for another few weeks. The marina is closed because of Mother Nature. Lake Yellowstone is still almost completely covered in ice. Once Lake Yellowstone thaws, the entire area will be bustling with activity.

Greg from Indiana State is a first time Yellowstone employee. He graduated only twenty days before the Lake Hotel opened. He had decided last Christmas he would try to get a job in Yellowstone for the Summer before venturing into the "real world" job market.

One of his women friends worked at Canyon last year and would be working in the Park again this year. She had given him some good advice on how to get hired. When Greg filled out his application he put on it he would accept one of the lousey jobs, like busser or dishwasher. When he got hired, he was under the impression that he would be working one of those jobs. Once he got to Lake Hotel he discovered he would be working in the Deli, down the hall from the registration desk. The Deli has a wonderful view of Lake Yellowstone, plus working in the Deli is an OK job with one major benefit. The Deli does not open til 10:30am, which means you do not have to get up at the crack of dawn.

The Lake Hotel is the oldest hotel in the Park, even older than the Inn at Old Faithful. Lake Hotel is elegant and distinguished. To stand in its magnificent lobby, you would never guess you are in a wilderness area. (To me this is NOT good. Give me a tent or a rustic shelter at Roosevelt when I am in Yellowstone.) The restaurant is superb with prices to match.

A Bell Porter or Waitstaff could make excellent tips here. Lake is where most V.I.P.s, politicians and movie stars will stay when they visit Yellowstone. Let me note this, I do love the Lake area but can you guess I think the fancy hotel should be somewhere else?

The Lake Yellowstone Cabins and Lake Lodge are close to the Hotel.

◆◆◆

Bridge Bay is a couple of miles from the Lake Hotel. Bridge Bay has a first class marina which rents paddle boats and fishing boats. The prices are very reasonable, which was a big surprise to me.

FISHING GUIDES are also available at Bridge Bay. I talked with two of the women GUIDES. I hoped to go fishing sometimes during the summer.

The DOCK HANDS work three long days then a half day, then they are off three and a half days.

Bridge Bay employees never leavel A lot of students that work here become school teachers so they can continue to work summers. THIS IS A FANTASTIC JOB!

From the Bridge Bay Marina you depart and return for the "scenic cruise". This is a boat trip approximatly two hours long. You ride out across the Lake, circle an island which is about half mile in size, and return to the marina. A lot of the Park employees refer to the scenic cruise as the "scenic snooze". That might be true if the tour consisted only of what I described above. One important bit of information has been left out. On the edge of the island is a Bald Eagle's nest!!

When my nephew John and I took the tour, we saw several Bald Eagles. The tour itself is really not as bad as it has been described, but add in the Bald Eagle sightings and the scenic cruise becomes a must-do event.

The opportunity to observe wildlife in their natural environment is reason enough to visit Yellowstone. Remember this, these animals are dangerous. They can and have killed people. Do not approach any animal and especially do not approach a Mother bear with her cub.

Last summer my nephew John and I were driving the six miles of Blacktail Plateau Drive. This is a beautiful but rarely visited area. As we drove, we came upon two other cars with guests stopped in front of us. Any time you see people stopped, observe where they are looking. You will most likely see an animal. We looked about two hundred yards in the distance and there was a most gorgeous, probably five hundred pound golden Grizzly. We observed it from the road for over ten minutes as three other cars pulled up behind us. We were all enjoying the Grizzly from the road when we noticed the man from the last car to pull up. He had gotten out his video camera and he and his six year old son were heading toward the Bear! Several other people besides me saw him at the same time. We began yelling at him to come back to the road. He made it clear with gestures we should mind our own business. I then whipped out my whistle, blew it loudly, and proclaimed a big lie. I said "Sir, I am with the National Park Service, and you must return to the road immediately." At once he became very polite and returned to his car.

I am confident the other guests approved of this action, even though the Bear disappeared into the woods. One man from a car in front of me came over to me, smiled and said "thanks Ranger". I could tell from the look on his face he knew I was just a guest like him. Maybe the Bear would not have attacked "Video-Man" and his son, but I am glad we will never find out.

Later John and I went to Cooke City for dinner. I told the Video-Man story to Ted from New York, our waiter. Ted said this man had not been the dumbest person in the Park that week. He had been told of a couple who had actually sat their very small child on top of a buffalo to take a picture. Luckily the child was unhurt when it fell as the Buffalo bolted and ran. Like I keep saying, "please be careful, these are wild animals."

The HOSPITAL for Yellowstone is located at Lake. Dial 911 for emergency help within the Park.

Lake, Grant and Canyon are in the southern part of the Park. They are not very convenient to any of the small towns near the Park's northern entrances. I mention in the chapters on Grant and Canyon that a lot of park employees go to Lake for nighttime comradeship. The Lake is a beautiful area in the daytime. This is enhanced even more with a shimmering moon.

I saw a lot of Lake, Grant and Canyon employees at both *Eino's* and K-Bar.

Wendy worked at the Lake Hamilton Store in the snack bar. When I asked her why she was working in Yellowstone, I got the very best answer anyone gave me. Wendy's answer will tell you in and of itself the outstanding character of this lady.

Wendy attends Stephen F. Austin University in Texas. She will be a Senior.

Both of her grandparents have spent their summers working in the Park for Hamilton the past ten years.

Sadly, Wendy's grandfather died in October. The loss to the family was tremendous.

In March, Hamilton contacted Wendy's grandmother to arrange the grandparents' summer jobs. Hamilton was told of the tragedy and offered both condolence and an offer for the grandmother to still come to Yellowstone and work. In most cases, when a spouse dies, the surviving spouse will not return to the Park.

Wendy was unaware of her grandmother's communications with Hamilton until one day her grandmother asked Wendy if she would go with her and work for Hamilton for the summer. An instant "YES" was the reply.

Wendy and her grandmother were "roomies" at Lake for the summer.

A footnote to this: I thought Wendy was probably the person in her family with all the charm and wit. Then I met her grandmother. What a fun person to be around!

Wendy and her grandmother, two wonderful people.

Mammoth

Mammoth Hot Springs is located five miles inside the Park's North entrance. Gardiner, Montana is located here at the Park's gateway. The Gardiner volunteer fire department is nicknamed the *Gateway Hose Company*. At this entrance is the famous Roosevelt Archway, etched with the quote by President Roosevelt, *"For the Benefit and Enjoyment of the People"*.

Be sure you do not confuse the North entrance Roosevelt archway with the archway over the corrals in the Roosevelt Lodge area. There have been several instances where a guest asking directions to the Roosevelt Archway was sent to the archway over the Roosevelt corrals. The arch at Roosevelt corrals is "an" archway, not "the" archway. Just remember, no one

Matt from Pittsburgh, one of the most respected friends many people have.

would want directions to see the archway over the Roosevelt corrals.

Mammoth Hot Springs is referred to as MAMMOTH by everyone. This is the area where the U.S. Army was originally stationed. The area was called Fort Yellowstone while the Army was stationed here.

Mammoth is Park Headquarters. It is opened to automobile traffic year round. After a major snowstorm you will probably need snow tires or chains to get from Gardiner to Mammoth. This is a steep and winding road. Even in good weather it can be dangerous. Be careful also because an elk or sheep could run in front of your car, especially at night.

The Post Office at Mammoth is open all year.

The Mammoth area also has a historical church. The church was built as part of Fort Yellowstone in the late 1800's.

The Clint Wilkes Original College Guide to a Summer Job In Yellowstone

The hotel at Mammoth is very comfortable. It offers rooms with or without bath. Just like at the Snow Lodge, you also have convenient women and men facilities to serve those rooms without baths.

Cabins are also available near the Mammoth Hotel. Some of the cabins have showers, others do not. Several shower facilities are conveniently located all around the cabin area.

The limestone terraces at Mammoth are beautiful in both the Winter and Summer. To get to the top of the terraces, the Park Service has built a series of walkways. If you walk easy it is about a twenty minute walk from the Hotel to the terrace area. To walk the entire terrace walkway should take about an hour. It is an uphill stairway to get to the top, but the walk is worth it. The walkways not only protect nature's investment, but they are for your safety. Be safe, stay on the walkways. You can also drive to the top of the terrace area. You will still need to walk a short distance to observe this wonder.

Many Park employees will hold their weddings in this church.

The Clint Wilkes Original College Guide to a Summer Job in Yellowstone

♦♦♦

The Mammoth corrals are located a short drive from the Hotel. Horseback rides are offered daily.

Amy from Montana is the Head Wrangler at Mammoth. She has been riding horses as long as she can remember.

♦♦♦

Employees at Mammoth go to Gardiner frequently. Gardiner is five miles away and offers a limited nightlife. The most recent attraction is *Outlaws,* the new Pizza Restaurant. The main draw is it has a salad bar. At Shawnee's recommendation, I had the Calazone and enjoyed it.

Shawnee has worked for T.W. Services for several years, ever since she got out of High School. She was actually born in Yellowstone. Her parents met many years ago when they were both Park employees working at Roosevelt. They moved to Livingston to raise a family, and Shawnee was born during one of their frequent trips to Yellowstone. When you call reservations you may be talking to Shawnee.

Outlaws may be good, but the best Pizza is at *K-Bar*. *K-Bar* is one of the more popular saloons for Park employees. I would sit in *K-Bar* many an afternoon typing away on this book. The two trucks parked on the street beside *K-Bar* have car tags reading *K-Bar* 1 and *K-Bar 2.*

Patty and Glen own *K-Bar.* They bought it a couple of years ago. Patty is one of the nicest ladies I have ever met. Her daughter, Shauna, is one of the four full-time barkeeps. The other three are Laura, Miss Marian, the pretty school marm, and Chadd. Patty works as a waitress and you would never know she was the owner unless you happen to ask. I did ask Patty if she was *K-Bar 1* or *K-Bar 2*. Her immediate reply was *K-Bar 1*.

The Author(left) with Dana and Chadd at K-Bar.

Mammoth is also closer than much of the rest of the Park to Livingston and Bozeman. I strongly recommend a trip to Montana State University in Bozeman to visit the Dinosaur museum.

Elk roam freely in the entire Mammoth area. They will even venture into the yards of Park Service employees.

Early morning and late afternoon are the best times to view animals. This is when they are feeding.

I met many room attendants at Mammoth who were enjoying their work. There were three roommates from Charleston College, Kristann, Lucy and Tammie. All of these women were very sharp! They had driven from the east coast via New Orleans up through my favorite city of Austin into Colorado, then up to Yellowstone. They had planned a two week trip to get to the Park.

In a few years if I need a bright Attorney, I plan to hire Tammie!

I was in the Best Western Bar in Gardiner watching game one of the N.B.A. Championship Series when I saw three familiar women with some of their friends. It was Lucy, Kristann and friends taking Tammie out to dinner to celebrate her twenty first birthday. I walked over said hello and happy birthday and bought them a round of desserts.

Since Tammie was off work the next day she was doing her best to celebrate her big event. Both Kristann and Lucy had to be back cleaning rooms at 8 A.M. the next day. All three of them had not been able to get the same two days off together. Tammie had Wednesday and Thursday for her "weekend". Kristann and Lucy had Thursday and Friday. They did all get Thursday off together and had gone white water rafting in Jackson Hole the week before.

Later in the summer, when more employees were hired, Tammie was able to switch her off days to cooridinate with her buddies.

◆◆◆

Mammoth has two Hamilton Stores. The store next to the Y.P.S.S. station is much like the other Hamilton Stores. It has gifts, groceries, microwave food and clothes. The other Hamilton store is very unique. It is a combination Christmas Gift Store and Photo Shop. This store is about half mile down the road as you go toward Roosevelt.

The Y.P.S.S. station is run by Mike from Minnesota. Another of the Park employees I met my first day in Yellowstone this year.

T.W. runs the hotel and cabins plus shops. A gift shop is located off the lobby of the hotel. Across from the hotel is a large building. The end of the building contains an upscale restaurant. The food is excellent. All three meals are served, with reservations needed for dinner.

The other end of the building contains a fast food restaurant and ice cream shop. I'll say the same thing for this fast food place as I say about them all. The hungrier you are, the better the food tastes.

The Clint Wilkes Original College Guide to a Summer Job in Yellowstone

Grand Canyon of Yellowstone

My first visit to CANYON was the Fall of 1987. Since the Summer rush was over, there were not a lot of people in the Park. I pulled my rental car into the nearly empty parking lot, unbuckled my seat belt and started to get out.

Before I opened my door, I noticed the biggest Crow I had ever seen standing only a few feet from my car. I decided I did not want to get out immediatly and now would be a good time to sit in my car and read the geyser brochures I had gotten back at Old Faithful. These brochures are not Shakespeare, and I had completed reading them in a few moments. The crow was still there.

The Clint Wilkes Original College Guide to a Summer Job in Yellowstone

I continued to sit in my car and ponder the situation. Even though this was my first trip to Yellowstone, I knew it would be a bad idea to try to do anything to frighten the crow away. The Park Rangers can become very upset if you attack any animal, even a two foot tall crow.

I thought I saw the solution when a station wagon pulled into the parking space two places to my left. The crow did not move. I then noticed two Japanese twin girls, about four years old, getting out of the back seat. Now what do I do? I do not speak Japanese and how was I to let these two girls and their parents know there was a gigantic crow ready at any moment to carry off their children.

I could not sit in my rental car while our Country's foreign relations with Japan were destroyed by this crow flying off with what were probably the Emperor's grandchildren.

I knew what I must do! I would save the children! I was about to become a hero!

I would probably get a reward, like a trip to Tokyo or at least a free oil change for my Honda.

I opened my door and headed toward the crow and the family. I think I understood the foreign language of one of the little girls as she approached the crow while holding her Mothers hand. In Japanese it had to have been "nice birdy". She tossed the crow part of a cookie and it flew off.

I was then still far enough away that they were not aware I was headed toward them to avert a world situation. I walked past them and proceeded toward the Grand Canyon of Yellowstone. Several American tourists were standing on the viewing platform. I overheard one of their conversations, something about the Park having lots of Eagles and RAVENS!!

The Clint Wilkes Original College Guide to a Summer Job in Yellowstone

❖❖❖

Most people are surprised to learn Canyon actually has more rooms than the Old Faithful area. Canyon has about 609 rooms, consisting mostly of cabins, except for the new thirty seven room hotel which opened summer 1993.

The cabins are spread out over three areas with parking fairly close to each unit. All of the cabins have bathrooms.

These cabins were built a long time ago. I heard in the 1950's. Their design was probably appreciated then.

The facilities at Canyon are within walking distance of the Grand Canyon of the Yellowstone. Even though it is a short walk, be careful and take your whistle.

Canyon is one of the areas with Corrals, which means they offer horseback rides. (Watch your step!)

The Wranglers are a remarkable group to be around. They are always telling tall tales and having fun. Their work looks like fun, but it is also one of the hardest jobs in the Park. Every Wrangler's first priority is taking care of their horse. A Wrangler may be worn out tired, but they will first make sure their horse is secure before calling it a day. Amazingly, after a shower and brief rest most Wranglers get a second wind and are ready to spend an evening with the company of their friends.

The National Park Service tries to always maintain a natural environment within the Park. Unless a human or a structure is in danger, the Rangers will not interfere with nature.

If a snag, (a dead tree), falls on a trail, the Park Service will only cut out that part of the tree which has fallen on the trail. When you are out walking you can clearly see where the Rangers have cut a section of tree to maintain a trail.

When an animal like a buffalo or elk dies in the middle of a trail the Rangers may close that trail. If it is a walking trail which is seldom used, the Rangers may create a new walking path around the dead animal. A trail used for the horseback rides would always be closed. The Rangers would not create a new trail to go around a dead buffalo. The destruction horse hoofs would cause could not be easily repaired.

Horseback trails are seldom closed. To close them would end those Wranglers' summer jobs in Yellowstone. The odds of an animal dying on the trail are enormous.

"Sliding buffalo" is one of the most remarkable phenomenon of our time. There is not a scientist in the world who has been able to explain this wonder of nature. What happens is this: A buffalo or elk which dies on a trail will mysteriously slide about twenty yards off the trail. In all accounts of other dead buffalo or elk which did not die on a trail you will find none of these mysterious slide marks.

I heard that several years ago, in a most unusual phenomenon, a buffalo was actually found to have slid from over one hundred yards off the trail onto the trail. Even more unusual was the buffalo had been dead for several days before it slid.

This occurred one day before this trail ride was scheduled to close. That very night a whole crew of Wranglers went to enjoy the nightlife of Jackson Hole.

There are many events of nature we will never understand, and I feel this is one we should never investigate.

◆◆◆

Canyon has a large Hamilton Store with a full service restaurant, ice cream shop, grocery store and gift shop. It also has a smaller photo shop nearby.

T.W. operates a full service restaurant. Helen, from France, works as a BUSSER. Kimberly, who will attend The University of Georgia this fall, works in the Ice Cream Shop located next to the Cafeteria.

I understand most employees usually go to the Corrals and visit with the Wranglers or go to Lake or *K-Bar* for nighttime entertainment.

◆◆◆

Elizabeth from Florida State University works in the T.W. gift shop at Canyon. She graduated in late April and had no idea a few weeks later she would be in Yellowstone.

Elizabeth majored in banking and was sure she would start her career the summer after graduation. She had several job offers which she would have gladly accepted until the job offer in Tampa was made. It was a much better offer than all the others. She said yes, fully expecting to start work as a Banker soon. As she went through her acceptance with the woman soon to be her boss, she found out she would not start her job in the new management program til September.

Elizabeth had a wonderful problem she had not expected. A summer off! That night she had dinner with her friends when one of them said, "why don't you work in Yellowstone this summer?" The friend had vaguely heard about college-age people working in the Park. Elizabeth called T.W. the next day and within a week had her job assignment at Canyon. She loves it!

Grant Village

The most recently built tourist area in the Park is Grant Village. GRANT, as it is called, was built in the mid 1980s to accommodate the many tour busses entering the Park. Grant has six lodges with over fifty rooms each.

This area was named after President Grant. It was President Grant who signed the legislation in 1872 naming Yellowstone the world's first National Park.

There is so much beauty in the Park it is truly unbelievable. When the Park was first discovered it actually was unbelievable. The early explorers to the area were not believed when they returned home and reported what they had seen.

The first "Mountain Men" to visit the Yellowstone area were known for telling "tall-tales". To say they had a credibility problem would be the kindest way to describe them. President Grant had to send an official expedition to verify all the claims of "smoking" ground and erupting water.

As you talk to people working in the Park, they can really make an impression on you. I remember one young lady, Carol from Nebraska, in particular. Carol was a front desk clerk at GRANT. I had talked to Carol a couple of times when I asked her " is this your first summer to work in the Park." She told me this was her fourth summer to work there, and it would be her last. She had passed the C.P.A. exam earlier in the year, and her parents wanted her to get a "real" job. Up until this point I had not realized a lot of students work in the Park for more than one summer.

The best job at Grant is definitely Bell Porter. Bell Porters make excellent tips carrying luggage. Most of the tour bus guests have pre-tipped as part of the tour cost.

Grant is near the South entrance of the Park. It is located near the West Thumb of Yellowstone Lake. The West Thumb thermal areas are interesting. There are mud pots and boiling water pools. They have great names like Black Pool, which is actually blue. There is a pool named Bluebell Pool which is blue. See Surging Spring and you will understand how it gets its name. The water surges up and overflows its dome. The Thumb Paint Pots, once the most visited thermal area at West Thumb, had been in decline. Recently, however, they have begun to again put on a show.

For guests, the best thing to do at Grant is to have a steak dinner at the Grant Steak House. The restaurant sits on the edge of Yellowstone Lake with a magnificent view. Reservations are not required at the Grant Steak House, but they are required at the other nice restaurant also on the Lake, located a short walk away.

One of the larger Hamilton Stores is located at Grant. It has a full service restaurant which employs over twenty college students. I talked to most of them and they say the tips are excellent.

One young man I talked with had a most outstanding attitude toward life. His name was Mike, he attends Duquesne University majoring in Political Science. He has "future leader" written all over him. As we talked I knew he could easily be a future Governor, Congressman or C.E.O.

Mike totally surprised me when he told me what he wanted to be. Mike wants to teach high school. His future students have much to look forward to!

Grant has several great places for laying out and catching rays next to Lake Yellowstone. I was completely surprised when I found out about them. They are available to the tourists, but mostly it's Park employees on the "beach". (Sunburns are a big concern...be careful.)

Like I have mentioned before, the water is freezing.

Employees at Grant usually go to Lake for nighttime entertainment.

This is the closest location to Jackson Hole, where many employees go on their days off. It is about seventy miles to Jackson Hole. There is a lot to do in Jackson Hole, but be prepared to spend a paycheck.

Grant is also close to Grand Teton National Park, which has an abundance of outdoor activities.

Hiking

In this chapter I am going to talk about a few of the hikes I went on.

If you do not know a lot about hiking, I suggest you read an excellent book by Cindy Ross called *"A HIKER'S COMPANION"*. It contains a lot of information for women which a male author would not think about, but it is an excellent source of information for both women and men.

Yellowstone is as full of danger as it is full of beauty. Even for a short hike you should carry some basic essentials for survival. First carry a friend; it is dangerous to hike alone. Always carry at least a day pack with water and a snack. Never drink all of your water, except in an emergency. The same holds true for the snack. You should carry extra of these two items for emergency use only.

You should keep your whistle in your pocket or on a string around your neck. If the whistle is in your backpack and you drop it off a cliff, then it can do you little good.

I always carry a walking stick with bear bells on it. I also put bear bells on my backpack. I am sure I sound like Mr. Christmas coming down the trail. Even so, I have seen hikers with twice as many bells as I have.

Consult the Park Ranger material for other essential items to carry. They will also encourage you to take a first aid kit, and I agree.

My two favorite hikes are the five mile hike from near Old Faithful to Lone Star Geyser and the five mile Beaver Ponds Loop hike from Mammoth.

The Lone Star Geyser hike requires a three mile drive from Old Faithful to get to the trail head. A trail head is the start of the trail. To drive to the trail head, depart Old Faithful and drive toward West Thumb. As soon as you approach Kepler Cascades, the Lone Star trail parking lot is just as you pass the south Kepler parking lot entrance.

This hike is on a well groomed, mostly flat gravel trail along side a small river. The route is two and a half miles from the trail head to the geyser, and you return via the same route. I like this hike because it is convenient to get to with very little preplanning.

Lone Star erupts about every three hours. Good luck on seeing it.

You can continue on the Lone Star geyser trail to several other destinations.

Because I spend a lot of time in Gardiner and at Mammoth, I frequently go on the Beaver Ponds loop hike. This is a hike I will take many mornings after breakfast. You make a horseshoe like loop on this hike. You can start on either end, either behind the Mammoth Hotel or at the Minerva Terraces. The two start/end trail heads are across a large parking lot from each other.

I prefer to start behind the Hotel. You begin with a fairly steep climb up a small hill. After this you encounter several small inclines for the next five miles. The last mile is downhill to the terraces. If you had started at the terraces, you would have to go uphill for the first mile. This is not my favorite way to start a hike.

I hike the Beaver Ponds trail alone, but I strongly recommend you do not hike alone. Always hike with one or more people. I was an infantryman in Vietnam with the 101st Airborne Division. I have had extensive training in traversing the wilds. Does this make it O.K. for me to hike alone? Absolutely not! I should hike with other people also, but many times I do not. I spend so much time talking with people I feel I need this time alone. This is not a good excuse, so when I get eaten by a bear it will be my fault!

The only problem I ever had on the Beaver Ponds trail was during my fourth time to hike it. I was carrying my walking stick with bear bells plus my backpack with bells.

The trail was posted by the Park Rangers with a warning of bears in the area. I had talked to several Park employees who told me of sightings of a mother bear with her cub. Bears are always dangerous, but they are most dangerous when they are defending their cubs.

Other times of extreme danger are if the bear is eating a carcass or if you surprise the bear by walking up on it from downwind. They would smell you if you were upwind. A bear's sense of smell is a thousand times stronger than a human's.

I figured if I rattled my bells on my stick I would

make enough noise the bear would hear them and avoid me. The plan was working well until I was a little over three-fourths through the hike. I had passed the beaver dam and was in a clearing near a wooded area.

From out of the woods appeared three college age people. Two males and one female. The two males had on t-shirts from a prominent university. The female I recognized from having met in a group of Park employees a couple of weeks prior.

From about fifty yards away, one of the men yelled, "hey, you *"so and so"*, you are making such *"so and so"* noise we could hear you from way back yonder." (I am using *"so and so"* to cover a variety of profane and most profound vocabulary).

They hurried toward me extremely upset. I was wanting to first calm them before trying to talk with them. I did not respond to further *"so and so"* comments till they got close. The lady told them twice to calm down as they approached me.

As they got closer, I sat down and opened my pack and got out my water. I had not yet responded to their taunts.

When they got to me they were still upset. I said, "howdy". This was not a response they expected. The lady seemed very embarrased by their behavior.

One of the men looked at my stick and said, "why do you have a *"so and so"* stick with bells on it?" I felt confident they were blowing steam and were not going to attack me. They calmed down but still demanded an explanation of why I was making so much *"so and so"* noise. I slowly explained these were bear bells so a bear would hear me coming and would avoid me. I told them a mother bear and her cub had been seen in the area.

I looked at the name of the great University and wondered if they were actually students or just supporters. Then I remembered even the best schools have morons. This school just happened to have what I discovered were two brothers, both morons, as students.

One did appear to be slightly brighter than the other. I named him Bright Boy. This one could say a sentence with only about half the profanity of the other.

They listened as I explained my bear bells story. This explanation did not help. Bright Boy proceeded to explain they were actually **looking** for the mother bear and cub. They wanted to get a picture to show their friends. They had one of those disposable cameras, which meant they would need to get very close to take any kind of decent picture.

The lady that was with them had not said anything until Bright Boy said they were actually **looking** for the bear. She said, in a harsh tone, she had not realized bears were in the area or that they were hunting bear. She did not have the look of a happy camper on her face.

I then asked both brothers what they would do if the bear started to chase them. Without a moment's hesitation they both replied, "run!".

The female was shocked by the reply. She looked at them and said. "Run!" "First, you are not supposed to run from a bear. It triggers their predator instinct, and second, are you saying you would run off and leave me?"

Bright Boy reflected on his answer, then said," we would not run off and leave you. I would fight the bear with this stick." As he held the feeble lodge pole pine stick he was not very convincing. The old joke about, "I don't have to outrun the bear, I just have to outrun you", seemed appropriate. I did not tell it.

The three of them then got into a heated discussion. All I could think of was; the state these two men were from needed stronger laws against cousins marrying.

The brothers were determined to find the bear. The lady was going to have no part of it. She asked if she could walk back with me. Neither Bright Boy nor his dumb-ass brother seemed to mind.

Bright Boy gave her his car keys to get her stuff out of the car.

The walk back was most enjoyable. The lady apologized immensely and told me how she vaguely knew these two guys from school. They did not know she was working in Yellowstone when they saw each other at Old Faithful. It was her off day, and a trip to Mammoth sounded like fun. She said they had seemed O.K. until they started all the cussing when they saw me from the edge of the woods.

She had already made plans that night to stay with friends working in Mammoth.

I walked with her to Bright Boy's car for her to get her purse and other items. She was supposed to leave the key on the top of the front tire.

I got a big laugh when she got her stuff, locked the car and took the key over to the bear-proof trash can and dropped it in. All she needed to say for an explanation was, "they would have run off and left me!"

The list of items the Park Rangers recommend you carry on a hike does not include a spare set of car keys.

Winter in Yellowstone

Winter in Yellowstone is completely different from the Summer experience. The Park is a true Winter Wonderland.

Only limited facilities are open in the Winter. The lodging facilities at Lake, Roosevelt, Grant and Canyon are closed.

The Season varies slightly at Old Faithful and Mammoth. These areas are open from about mid December to mid March. Call the Park Service for exact dates.

The Park Service grooms some of the Park roads for use by snowmobiles. You can rent a snowmobile from T.W. at the Snow Lodge or Mammoth Hotel or from other

A bear-proof trash can next to an outhouse

companies outside the Park. You can even bring your own snowmobile. A valid drivers license is required to operate a snowmobile inside the Park.

Up until the Winter of 1993-94, the Park Service would allow snowmobiles to be driven by anyone over the age of twelve. These drivers were suppose to stay close to another snowmobile being driven by an adult. Records over the years have shown these young drivers were involved in a large percentage of the snowmobile accidents in the Park.

Every winter employee I have talked with has a horror story about something incredibly stupid being done by an adult on a snowmobile.

Snowmobiles are a lot of fun, but they are extremely dangerous. Operate them with care.

The areas which are open need staffing in Winter the same as Summer. HOUSEKEEPING, ACCOUNTING, FRONT DESK CLERK and all the jobs in the RESTAURANTS are needed in Winter.

The Old Faithful area is open. The Snow Lodge and cabins are open. The Lodge and Inn at Old Faithful are closed.

The Old Faithful area has a fast food restaurant open all day during Winter. The Snow Lodge restaurant is open for breakfast, lunch and dinner. A small gift shop is located in the Snow Lodge Lobby.

A ski shop is open next to the Snow Lodge. Skis and snowshoes are available for rent. Expert instructors are available for cross country ski lessons.

Last Winter when I was interviewing Park employees, one name kept coming up. George! Everyone said I should meet George.

I met George and, even though I had been to Yellowstone on six previous trips, I now feel the experience is complete. George personifies the type of person working in Yellowstone—someone who absolutely loves Yellowstone. George has worked in the Park for many years. When I met him, he was in the Dispatch office at the Snow Lodge. This job requires coordinating the snow coach drivers as they travel about the Park. George was extremely busy as I talked with him in his office. At one point I referred to his operation as the "brain-center" of the Park. He was quick to correct me and said a more accurate observation would probably be the "funny-bone".

The HAMILTON STORE at MAMMOTH is open year round to serve the Park Ranger community. Alice, who now works for Hamilton Stores, has worked in the Park since 1947.

Yellowstone Park Service Stations operates several

service areas in the Winter for snowmobiles. They have limited spare parts. They do not offer snowmobile repair services. Snowmobile fuel is available at Canyon, Fishing Bridge, Old Faithful and Mammoth. Be sure you check with a Park Ranger or Y.P.S.S. to find operating hours for snowmobile fueling stations and locations of warming huts. Contact Y.P.S.S. in Gardiner to check on jobs available.

The NORTH ENTRANCE is open year round. This is the entrance to the Mammoth area. The Park Service keeps the NORTH entrance open to allow the Park Service employees access to Gardiner and the outside world. They also maintain the road from Cooke City to Mammoth In Winter. This road can be treacherous under the best conditions.

The MAMMOTH HOTEL is open during the Winter season, which varies slightly each year from about mid December to mid March. The Hotel has a gift shop in the Lobby.

In front of the Hotel is a full service restaurant, open for breakfast, lunch and dinner. Dinner reservations are required. A fast food restaurant is adjacent to the full service restaurant.

The Mammoth Hotel also has a cabin with a hot tub. Rental is available on an hourly basis. This is near the ice skating area behind the hotel. Skis, ice skates and snowshoes are available for rent. Mammoth also has expert ski instructors available.

The only road in the Park open to cars in the Winter is the road from Gardiner up to Mammoth and over to Cooke City.

The West entrance is open to snowmobiles and snowcoaches. The South entrance is open to snowcoaches and snowmobiles from Flagg Ranch. You can access some of the road areas in the rest of the Park via snowmobile and snowcoach. This is all subject to Winter weather conditions and Park Service approval.

Jobs in Winter are very difficult to get. Most of the Winter jobs are taken by people who worked in the Summer and want to spend a Winter in the Park. It is common for a Winter employee to have worked several Summers and to even be in their third, fifth or tenth Winter. Many of the Winter employees performing jobs such as BUSSER or GIFT SHOP CLERK are actually Managers and high ranking Summer employees. They love Yellowstone so much they will work at any job available. I also have met several Park Rangers who get laid off at the end of the Summer season, so in the Winter they work for one of the Park concessionaires.

The Winter employees are a special group. Many I talked with were the daughters and sons of former employees or the younger sister or brother of a former employee.

Having said all of that, I did hear of some first timers working in the Park last Winter. You can only find out if a job is available by asking.

A few of the jobs available only in the Winter are, of course, directly related to the Snow, such as SKI INSTRUCTORS. Yellowstone has fantastic cross country skiing.

SNOWCOACH DRIVER. Do you know what a Bombardier is? This is a type of snowcoach which is used to transport guests on tours and ski trips. They also have snow-vans, which are vans with snow tracks instead of tires. In the summer they are converted to normal vans.

Try to take a tour with Bryan, from Oregon, in either the Winter or Summer. He does great imitations of Elk, Bison and snowmobiles. All of the tours I went on had great guides, but Bryan was the best.

SNOWMOBILE RENTER. T.W. rents a lot of snowmobiles every day in the Winter. Someone must issue the winter clothing and give instructions in snowmobile operation.

The RESERVATIONS department has about a dozen Winter employees compared to over fifty in the Summer.

There are several WARMING HUTS open which sell microwave food and hot drinks during limited hours of operation. There is one at Madison, one at Canyon and one at West Thumb. Check with the Park Service for safety ideas and other facilities.

Yellowstone in Winter can be dangerous with the extremes in weather. Contact the Park Service for complete information for your safety. The Park Rangers' phone number is (307) 344-7381. (Inside Yellowstone: Dial 911)

Working Near Yellowstone

I will name only a few businesses in each town. I will give the address and phone number (if available) of the Chamber of Commerce for each place. They will send you a list of member businesses with addresses and phone numbers.

If you call you can find out about the opportunities available.

WEST YELLOWSTONE
    West Yellowstone is full of restaurants, hotels and t-shirt shops. There are many places for RVs and tenters. All of these need summer employees.
    Some of the businesses in West will provide lodging

for employees. You will need to contact each employer to find out their policy.

The Madison Youth Hostel is worth a visit. You can stay there even if you are not a youth. The lobby is full of interesting artifacts and old Yellowstone pictures. The Madison is the oldest hotel in West. President Harding stayed here when he visited the Park. You are welcome to tour the hotel; the owners may even serve as your guide.

◆◆◆

The StageCoach Inn is owned and operated by Hamilton Stores Inc. It is a full service hotel with a restaurant and a bar. During the summer they have a downstairs nightclub with live bands on weekends. They need a full compliment of employees during the summer. Apply through the Hamilton Stores Personnel Office in West Yellowstone.

Even if you work somewhere else or are just visiting West, ask to see one of the StageCoach Inn rooms. The designer deserves an award for the way they have decorated these rooms!

◆◆◆

The Gusher is an excellent Pizza restaurant. On Wednesday nights they have "all you can eat" spaghetti. This is the only time they serve spaghetti. They need to add it to the menu!

Campfire Lodge is great for breakfast or lunch. Nancy, Teresa and Chuck are wonderful hosts.

Chamber of Commerce
100 Yellowstone Ave.
West Yellowstone, Montana 59758
1-406-646-7701

JACKSON HOLE

You will definitely want to visit Jackson Hole during your summer in Yellowstone. You may want to work in Jackson Hole. They have plenty of jobs available during the summer.

The housing problem for summer employees is worse, if that is possible, in Jackson Hole than other towns. You may be able to find a place but be prepared to pay out the kizoo.

The "Fashion Police" which do not exist in Yellowstone are in full force and working overtime in Jackson Hole. A lot of people still wear their "grubbies", but most people dress like the cover of Glamour or GQ.

Jackson Hole is full of great places. The new BrewPub serves several varieties of their own beer, plus great food.

Lisa, a Texan attending Richmond College, works at a great pizza place. Mountain High Pizza Pie has some of the best pizza I have ever tasted.

Jackson Hole is full of stores to shop in. The Jack Dennis store carries almost everything from hiking supplies to t-shirts. I bought a lot of both from New Orleans native, Elizabeth, a senior at "Roll Tide, Alabama".

Elizabeth, "Roll Tide"

Chamber of Commerce
P.O. Box E
Jackson Hole, Wyoming 83001

SILVER GATE AND COOKE CITY

Silver Gate is located one mile from the Northeast entrance. It has a few hotels, gift shops and restaurants.

Chamber of Commerce
Silver Gate, Montana 59020

Cooke City is located about four miles from the Northeast entrance. This entrance will lead you over the Beartooth Highway. Of the many gorgeous roads leading to Yellowstone, this is one of the most gorgeous. It is also one of the most interesting. The road does not open until the snow melts. Sometimes as late as early June. It will close for the winter with the first major snowfall in September or October.

Cooke City has hotels, restaurants, and gift shops which need employees. Some of the employers provide housing for employees. Since Cooke City is so isolated they just about have to provide housing. The housing provided could best be described as primitive.

One of the more interesting people I met worked in Cooke City. Her name is Wendy and she attends computer college in Maryland. She lived in a small room behind Joan & Bill's, "The Pie Place" with her friend since junior high, Tonya. They were both waitresses in Cooke City.

The day I met Wendy I liked her at once. She has the most friendly smile I have ever seen.

She had just gone through a series of incidents. First her rear window had been broken out when her bike rack was jarred loose as she hit one of Yellowstone's famous potholes. Then some yo-yo stole her car later that day. The yo-yo was allegedly an escaped soldier from Fort Levenworth. They caught him as he was leaving the Park a couple of days later.

I heard he was arrested while wearing several items of clothes Wendy had left in the car. One was her favorite t-shirt and the others were not items you would expect a male soldier to wear!

◆◆◆

Chamber of Commerce
P.O. Box 1146
Cooke City, Montana 59020

GARDINER

Gardiner, Montana is located at the north Yellowstone entrance. It is not yet as commercialized as West. It does have many shops, restaurants and hotels which need summer workers. Housing is close to non existent.

K-Bar is in Gardiner. I strongly recommend it for a casual lunch or dinner or just a game of pool.

Chamber of Commerce
P.O.Box 81
Gardiner, Montana 59030

GRAND TETON NATIONAL PARK

Grand Teton National Park is located directly south of Yellowstone. The few miles between the two parks are connected by the Rockefeller Parkway. The same entrance pass is accepted at both Yellowstone and Grand Teton National Park.

The original inhabitants, the Indians, called the Grand Teton Mountain Range "Teewinot", which means "Many Pinnacles". The early French explorers gave these majestic mountains the name "Les Trois Tetons". I debated whether or not to mention how the French explorers came up with this name or to write what these Frenchmen meant by the name. I chose the latter.

Remember, early French explorers were not politically correct!

The Teton Mountain Range has three large pointed mountains as their main attraction. As you look west from Jackson Hole the Tetons zoom skyward from a starkly contrasting flat plain. These early French explorers drew a conclusion in their minds that these three mountains looked like three grand breasts, "Les Trois Tetons", or translated, The Grand Tetons!

Another politically incorrect name from this era was the early ship, the "Cutty Sark". A cutty sark was actually a woman's slip or undergarment. In that day, the ship named "Cutty Sark" was considered very risque and daring.

Grand Teton Lodge Company
P.O. Box 240
Grand Teton Park, Wyoming 83013
1-307-543-2811

The Clint Wilkes Original College Guide to a Summer Job in Yellowstone

Mean People Suck!

Wendy from Maryland has a bumper sticker on her car which says, "MEAN PEOPLE SUCK." What a true statement this is! Almost everyone I met during my summer in Yellowstone was terrific. Unfortunatly there are always a few mean people no matter where you go. This brief chapter will tell of a few mean people who suck.

Wendy's bumper sticker saved her from getting a speeding ticket as she drove from Maryland to Yellowstone.

Wendy was doing eighty in a sixty five speed zone as she drove through Ohio. A Ohio State Trooper pulled her over and asked for her driver's license. He looked at it and said, "You need to slow down, young lady," and as he handed her license back to her, he said, "you are right, mean people do suck!"

It is hard for me to believe anyone would come to Yellowstone and do something mean. However, we do live in the real world and mean people are a part of it.

Most of the damage people do in Yellowstone is unintentional. They think it is O.K. to just take one rock as a souvenir, or I'll only walk a little ways in this restricted area, it can't hurt for one person to do this. You have many people thinking they are the only person picking a flower or getting off the trail.

These are what I refer to as non-thinking mistakes. I know about them, I did them too. We all will be a Touron at some point during the summer. When I saw a bear you can bet I stopped my car in the middle of the road and got out to take pictures!

Several years ago vandals actually took tree branches and rocks and stopped up a geyser located in the back country. They were never caught. They are the first winner of my "MEAN PEOPLE SUCK" award.

I started the hike up Mt. Washburn about ten o'clock one morning. It was a perfect late June day.

There was not a cloud in sight, and I knew this would be a great day to work on my tan as I hiked. I was carrying my t-shirt in my hand. (Be careful not to get burned).

The hike up Mt. Washburn is a steady uphill walk. You are walking on a dirt and gravel road. During most of the hike you will have your destination in sight. A Ranger fire watch station sits below the glass enclosed tourist viewing area on top.

The Clint Wilkes Original College Guide to a Summer Job in Yellowstone

A Ranger is on duty all summer on top of Mt. Washburn. The job of this Ranger is to watch for fires. He or she is rarely seen by the tourist. Many fires tourists will never hear about will burn in Yellowstone during the summer. They may be in remote areas. This Ranger station is a key part of monitoring these fires.

As I started my hike up Mt. Washburn, I realized I had made a terrible mistake. Since I was planning to get a tan, I had not worn my backpack. My water bottle was in my backpack!

I had drunk a pint bottle of orange juice with my granola bars early that morning. I first realized I was a tiny bit thirsty after about fifty minutes of the three mile hike. As I gained altitude, combined with continuous uphill walking, I was getting real thirsty. I could see a rest bench close in front of me. I needed to evaluate my situation.

I was about half way from the top. It takes about two hours to reach the top but only about one hour to get down. From where I was I could return to my car in about twenty five minutes. If water was available at the top I could make the entire hike. I had hiked this with my nephew John the previous summer. I could not remember if there was water at the top.

As I sat on the bench pondering my dilemma, two hikers were coming down the trail. As they approached, I asked them if there was a water fountain at the top. They replied "no, there is not a water fountain and we are out of water or you could have some of ours."

I had not thought about asking someone for a drink of water. I looked and saw three hikers coming up the trail, but I was not about to ask someone going UP the trail for water. I saw two hikers coming down the trail. I thought it might be O.K. to ask if they had any water since they were coming down.

As they approached I could see it was a mother and daughter. As they got close I asked them, " may I please have some water, if you have any left?"

I could understand a "no" answer if they had said they were out of water or only had a little left and planned to drink it.

The mother looked at me as I asked. She said nothing. What she did do instead of saying something stunned me. SHE LAUGHED! The kind of laugh that says, "I have plenty of water and I am not going to share a drop with you."

I am rarely at a loss for words. This was one of the rudest encounters I had ever had!

I sat for a few more minutes and could see more hikers coming down the hill. I could not imagine being rebuked again. Instead of waiting on them, I decided to end my hike and return to my car with its quart bottle and half gallon bottles of water.

The rude mother/daughter combo was over one hundred yards in front of me. They finished the hike and were in the parking lot with several other people. I had to walk past them to get to my car.

I started not to stop when I passed.....no, that's not true: I had every intention of stopping when I saw them.

I stopped, looked at all of them, and said, "I'm spending the summer in Yellowstone writing a book. When you read the story about the lady who laughed at me when I asked for water, (I then stared directly at this horrible person and said), "that will be you, lady!"

As I walked off, I heard the little girl say, "Mom, we had a lot of water left."

This lady earned a "MEAN PEOPLE SUCK" award.

◆◆◆

There may be more than one mean management person in Yellowstone, but I only met one. Everyone else I met was more than considerate, they were a pleasure to talk with.

I am sure this idiot's boss is not aware how he treats people or they would fire him on the spot.

Every company has people in management positions who will take advantage of their authority to demean and degrade others. This guy tops the list. You can only imagine how happy it must make his sick mind to make people miserable in Yellowstone!

My attorney told me if I identified this jerk in any way I could wind up getting sued. This guy is stupid enough to claim to be the "ass" and to sue me.

Well, Mr. Scatface, you and I know who you are and you get one of my "MEAN PEOPLE SUCK" awards.

Poachers in Yellowstone? Impossible?

No, it is not impossible. Every year irresponsible hunters are arrested for hunting inside the Park.

Probably 99% of hunters obey the rules of hunting. These hunters are the ones who pay the fees which enable us to save the habitat of wildlife.

The other 1%, especially the ones who hunt in Yellowstone, definitely deserve a "MEAN PEOPLE SUCK" award.

A lot of tourists will bring their pets with them to Yellowstone. I think those pet owners who bring their pets are terrific, if they take responsible care of the pet.

During my summer in Yellowstone, I saw the same sad situation repeated many times. A pet left locked in a hot car. These pet owners definitely deserve a "MEAN PEOPLE SUCK" award.

The worst situation I encountered was one Sunday morning while I had breakfast in West. I parked my car in front of an R.V. A small puppy was tied on a leash to the passenger door. The puppy was pacing the sidewalk waiting for its owner.

I ordered breakfast and went back out to get a newspaper. The puppy was barking like something was wrong. It had gotten its leash caught under the tire and, even though it was not being hurt, it was in a position where it could only stand in one place. I, along with a couple from Louisiana, approached to free the puppy. It started growling and would not let us near. We guessed we would scare it more if we tried to pick it up. We could see it was not injured, and we figured the owner would be back soon.

I returned to the restaurant, ate breakfast and read the Sunday paper.

The first thing I heard when I stepped out of the restaurant was the puppy barking. It had been over forty five minutes and the owner had not returned!

Several people tried to approach the puppy to free its leash. Each was unsuccessful.

I straightened out my tent and camping equipment I had tossed in the trunk that morning. The puppy continued barking as I worked.

After fifteen minutes I saw a man and his son walk toward me from around the corner. They began to run forward to the R.V. as soon as they heard the barking.

They got to the puppy and released his leash from under the tire.

Of course I had to say something!

They were only a few feet from me as I worked on

my camping equipment in my trunk. I looked at the man and said, "someone just went to call the police because that dog has been stuck for over an hour." The man looked at me and said it had not been an hour, only a few minutes. I stated how the dog had been stuck the entire time I had been at breakfast and how several of us had tried to get near it to free the leash.

The man became very angry, and said, "where are you from?" The question surprised me; it was not a question I expected. I closed my trunk, showing my Texas car tag. He looked at the tag and said, "Texas women are "*so and so's*". I desperately wanted to return a rude comment. Instead I said, "that's a real nice thing to say in front of your son!" He turned away and got in his R.V. I hoped he was not about to run over me! He pulled out and drove away.

I would bet the man loves his puppy. I am sure he never thought the puppy would get its leash stuck. That was just a mistake we all are capable of making.

This man deserves a "MEAN PEOPLE SUCK" award for his rude comment about Texas women.

Yellowstone is not an amusement park, but some people act like it is. They think you can trash the place and someone will clean up the mess they leave behind.

With over three million visitors each year, some trash is going to be accidentally spilled in the Park. The people that do this are usually careless, not mean. Most visitors would never purposely trash Yellowstone.

I now give a "MEAN PEOPLE SUCK" award to an entire family.

I was getting my backpack out of the trunk when a

family of five pulled in next to me. We were in front of the Inn. As the three kids got out they were tossing soda cans and candy wrappers on the ground. I looked at the parents and asked them to stop their kids from trashing the area. They both looked at me in astonishment and said, "Someone will clean it up, just like they do at Six Flags". One kid stuck out his tongue at me, one gave me half a peace sign, and the other kid said something which I am not real sure I know the exact meaning of so I had better not repeat it.

As they left, I picked up the trash and went to dispose of it. I had to go past the back of their car. On the bumper was a bumper sticker which said, "My Kid Can Beat Up Your Honor Student."

Animals

Yellowstone is not a drive through zoo. A lot of tourists do not understand this and will treat the animals like pets. A lot of tourists are injured every year!

◆◆◆

The Park employees I met all loved talking with me about the animals. Debbie from Michigan State was very helpful.

◆◆◆

Usually, an animal will stay in its own particular part of the Park, but do not be surprised to see any animal anywhere.

◆◆◆

The Clint Wilkes Original College Guide to a Summer Job in Yellowstone

The one animal all guests to Yellowstone want to see is the Bear. Yellowstone has two types of Bears; Black Bears and Grizzly Bears. I was told the difference between them is this: A Black Bear will climb a tree to eat you, and a Grizzly Bear will knock the tree down to eat you! Observe bears from a safe distance. Refer to the Park Ranger safety guides about Bear safety. Bears are my favorite animal in Yellowstone, with the Moose running a close second.

Before I tell the funniest story I heard about bears, let me explain about scat. If you are out hiking and see a pile of fresh scat, you should be aware a bear is nearby. You do not want to see a bear while hiking! Make noise and be very alert. It is true, a bear does scat in the woods.

Now for the story. A bear and a rabbit were following the call of nature one afternoon. The bear looked over at the rabbit and asked him if scat stuck to his fur. The rabbit replied, "no, it does not". So the bear finished his business, then picked up the rabbit and used him for toilet paper!

◆◆◆

I awoke early one morning to drive from Old Faithful to West. The sun was only a brightness on the horizon. I rounded a curve at thirty miles per hour and saw a moose about two hundred yards directly in front of me. I came to a stop and waited. The moose left the road and walked slowly down the hill by the road. I inched my car forward to about the spot where the moose had left the road. I got my camera and stepped out of my car to look down the hill. It was incredible, there were two moose grazing near a stream at the foot of the hill. I stayed there for almost an hour. I took my entire twenty four picture roll of black and white film, reloaded with color film and proceeded to take twenty more pictures before the two moose slowly walked away.

Later in the summer, again during early morning, I saw a mother moose with her baby moose playing in a pond. Two weeks later in this same pond I was fortunate enough to see three adult moose. Events like this will always "make your day".

A Moose has been described as looking like it was designed by a committee. Every part of a Moose's body looks inappropriate. Actually, a Moose has a very functional design. Long legs for walking in water and a large size for strength and protection.

Two moose

Watch carefully to observe animals, what you see is not always what you think it is—let me explain.

Let's say you are driving along beside the Yellowstone River. You look out and are certain you see a River Otter. When you stop your car for a better view, you notice the

Otter has not moved. You observe closely and see it is not really an Otter, it is a rock!

These are referred to as "Rock" Otters. Every animal in the Park has an exact duplicate rock twin. At some point during your stay in Yellowstone you will observe an animal in the distance which will turn out to be a rock. (I promised Amanda from Georgia I would put this story in the book.)

The coyote is one of the more intelligent animals in Yellowstone. If you do see a coyote, observe quickly. These are shy animals and will disappear when they see you.

A rarely seen animal is the Mountain Lion.

Elks are the most commonly seen animals. They will venture into many guest areas. Please ask anyone you

A pronghorn through my rear window

see approaching or feeding an Elk to refrain for the good of the Elk.

When you hike up Mount Washborn, you will have an excellent opportunity to view Bighorn Sheep. This hike takes a couple of hours. A herd of sheep can usually be observed when you get closer to the top of the mountain. (Be sure to take plenty of water.)

Watch fast to see a Pronghorn. The Indians used to say they are born running and seldom slow down.

Yellowstone is a home for the Red Fox, the Long Tailed Weasel, the Least Chipmonk, the Yellow-Bellied Marmot, several types of squirrels, the Pika, the Snowshoe Hare, Jack Rabbits, Muskrats, Beavers and Porcupines.

The Hamilton Store at Tower Falls is always busy. Several families of squirrels live here. Unfortunately, many Tourons like to feed them because they think they look cute standing on their hind legs begging for food.

One day I observed a grown man Touron feeding ice cream off his spoon to several squirrels. Most of the people watching thought this was a cute sight. The video cameras were numerous. An intelligent lady went up to the man and asked him not to feed the animals. He told her, translated to appropriate language, to "get lost." Several other Touron clones joined him in telling her to "get lost."

I walked over as the lady was leaving and motioned her to step over near us as I talked to the man. I asked him, "who is going to feed the squirrels on September 19?" This was mid-June, and he gave me a puzzled look and asked what was I talking about. I told him since he and other guests (Tourons) would be feeding the squirrels all summer, then they would not learn how to hunt their own food. So, who will feed them September 19, the day that Hamilton Store closed?

This man went ballistic!! He said "how dare you ask me that." I then replied that on September 26, about a week after the Hamilton Store closes, most of those squirrels will die of starvation.

The man definitely wanted to punch my lights out! He settled for storming off and driving away.

Should I have said what I did? I'm glad I did.

◆◆◆

In the Mammal family, I have saved the Bison to talk about last. It is O.K. to call a Bison a Buffalo, even though Buffalo is actually a name for the animal which looks somewhat similar, found in Africa. Everyone still calls the Bison a Buffalo. Who ever heard of "Bison" Bill Cody anyway?

When Park employees are travelling in Yellowstone and see a Touron road block ahead of them their first comments will always be, "look, a buffalo."

During a visit to Yellowstone, people do not realize when they first arrive that they will see a LOT of buffalo. During their first day or two, when they see a buffalo five hundred yards in the distance, they will stop in the middle of the road and grab their camera. After a few days, tourists become accustomed to seeing Buffalo. However, in Yellowstone, you always have new people arriving every day. Thus, "look, a buffalo!"

Bison do not want to be patted on the head! Be warned, Bison are dangerous. Do not approach! If a Bison raises its tail, it is going to definitely do one of two things. It is either going to charge or discharge. You do not want to be close if it does either one!

When the West was settled, the Bison were slaughtered in the millions. Thanks to efforts over the past fifty years, we have begun to save this species. Some Bison are still shot when they wander outside the Park boundaries. Bison may carry a disease which could be spread to cattle and do serious harm to the cattle business. For this reason the Bison who leave the Park must be destroyed.

I have seen a "Bison Hunt" on television. A hunter got up at dawn, dressed up in camoflauge fatigues, and had a guide take him to the Bison. The fearless hunter, from about fifty yards away, took aim and shot the Bison through the heart. This particular hunter was very proud of his deed.

Since you probably missed this show on television, let me tell you what really happened. The Bison was not hiding; he was just standing in place munching on grass. This would be a lot like going out in the parking lot on campus and shooting one of your friends' trucks. I have seen film where one Bison in a group was shot and the other Bison did not even run away.

I have nothing against hunting, nor do I oppose destroying the Bison which leave the Park, to save the cattle business. All I ask is, "Please do not call this hunting."

◆◆◆

Yellowstone is home to many birds. The most popular are the Trumpeter Swan and the Bald Eagle. Also keep alert to see a Pelican or Heron. Grouse, Hummingbirds, Nutcrackers, Jay, Magpie and Chickadee make a home in the Park.

Yellowstone is a home to Canada Geese. I made the mistake of calling them Canadian Geese in front of Ed from New Hampshire, one of our excellent tour guides.

The Clint Wilkes Original College Guide to a Summer Job in Yellowstone

This is incorrect. Ed explained, in a very nice manner, the Geese did not get the name Canada in reference to our neighbors from the North. Canada was the man's name who discovered this species.

Be sure to observe an American Dipper. They will dive to the bottom of the river and walk around looking for food. Watch as they go under. They will come up near the same spot in a short time.

Owls live in Yellowstone all year.

Many other birds also have a home in Yellowstone.

Yellowstone is also the home to lizards and frogs.

The Garter Snake is seldom seen but does live in the Park's lower elevations. Several other types of snakes also reside in the Grand Teton and Yellowstone area.

Fly fishing is great in Yellowstone. Cutthroat Trout are the only original fish in the Park. The other fish were introduced later by the Park Service for the benefit of fishermen.

◆◆◆

I have mentioned all through the book to be careful of the animals. It is very important for you to also be aware of people. Thieves can be in Yellowstone as easily as they can be on campus.

During her first Summer, Tracy had borrowed one of my favorite Alaska sweatshirts. It was stolen out of a washing machine while it was washing.

Tracy had spilled hot chocolate on it. The stain had not come out on two previous washings.

The thief was caught a few days later when Tracy and Ward, a Wrangler at Canyon and a real cowboy from Texas, saw a guy in an Alaska sweatshirt. It had a hot chocolate stain and looked exactly like the one I had loaned Tracy.

I always write my name in small letters somewhere on the inside of my sweatshirts. Tracy knew this and told Ward, who then approached the thief. Ward said something to the effect, "you had better be from Alaska and *your* name had better be written in that sweatshirt." A moment later the bare-chested, scared, but unhurt thief was walking away.

I have heard Ward is now a Texas Ranger, and I am sure he no longer uses these procedures when he is questioning a suspect.

None of this is meant to alarm, just be smart around animals and people.

◆◆◆

Read the booklets the Park Service provides concerning safety. They are for your benefit.

The Clint Wilkes Original College Guide to a Summer Job in Yellowstone

The Fires of '88

My first visit to the Park was in 1987. In 1988, Yellowstone experienced the largest fires recorded by man since becoming a National Park in 1872.

During late summer and early Fall 1988, Yellowstone was engulfed in fires which burned over one-third of the wooded area within the Park.

Some tourists will actually ask, "looks like there was a fire here recently, was there?" This would not be funny except it is Americans who ask this!

The fires were sickening to me as I watched them on television. I know it must be difficult for Tom Brokaw of NBC News, as he must sometimes report a horrible story. As Mr. Brokaw reported the Yellowstone fires night after night, I could see a look of anguish on his face. I understand he has a love for Yellowstone, like so many of us who have had an opportunity to visit the Park.

The Clint Wilkes Original College Guide to a Summer Job in Yellowstone

The efforts of the women and men Fire Fighters were truly heroic. My brother-in-law, Dale, is a Fire Fighter, so I hope this does not sound biased. I think being a Fire Fighter is one of the most courageous jobs there is. On the road to Cody, about twenty miles outside the Park, is a wonderful monument to Fire Fighters.

The second trip I made to the Park was in 1989, one year after the fires. Was I ever amazed! The Park was still beautiful! Yes, there were burned areas, but not like a burned city after a riot or a bombed area after a battle. Nature had already begun renewing itself. Where there were burned trees, there was already new growth. As it turns out, we discover Nature uses fire to get rid of the old trees and brush and bring in new growth. Those of us who were so sadden by the fires' destruction did not understand the vital role fire plays in nature.

Very few animals were killed in the fires. Unlike the movie *BAMBI*, the animals did not panic and run. Almost immediately after a fire swept thru an area, animals were seen returning to that same area, even though it was still hot and smoking,

Over thirty percent of the Park was affected by the fires. The only physical damage was to a few cabins in the Old Faithful area.

How can I say a few cabins were the only damage when over thirty percent of the Park was burned? We need to look at the role fire plays in Yellowstone to understand this. In order for Yellowstone to renew itself it must have fire. The Lodgepole Pine tree covers areas over most of Yellowstone. This tree must have fire to reproduce. The pine cone of a Lodgepole Pine must be heated to over 140 degrees to release its seed. Summers in Yellowstone are very cool, which leaves fire as the only source of heat to help the Lodge Pole Pine release its seeds.

Once the Lodgepole reaches maturity, it blocks the sun from the forest floor, causing almost all plants on the ground to die out. Without fires, Yellowstone would choke itself to death. The results of the fires were the reintroduction of many plant species. These plants had seeds in the ground which had been dormant for who knows how long.

We also have been able to study the rings of older trees, indicating major fires have swept thru Yellowstone about every three hundred years. The fires of "88" were actually "on time" for the natural procession of the area.

Let me give you a brief scenario of the events of 1988.

May of 1988 was one of the wettest months of May in the history of the Park. In June and July the Park had almost no rain.

Several fires were started by lightning and were allowed to burn themselves out. This "let burn" policy had been implemented years earlier to allow the Park to remain in its natural state. Only man-made fires were contained. In August and through the Fall, larger fires overtook the Park. Some of these fires actually started outside the Park boundaries and burned into the Park.

The Park Service made a decision to try to put out the fires. Everything the Park Service did was logical for the situation. Unfortunately, some politicians and bureaucrats became involved with bad suggestions which could have killed a lot of brave Fire Fighters. These suggestions also would have caused damage to the Park which would have taken lifetimes to repair.

Some politicians were wanting to send the Fire Fighters into the wilderness to fight the fires up close. The environment was uncontrolled fires with walls of flame over two hundred feet tall. This would have been impossible to fight while putting the brave women and men Fire Fighters in grave danger.

Another bad idea offered by the bureaucrats involved bringing in heavy equipment to cut out huge areas of forest. This would have left permanent scars in the Park for generations, and would have been useless as fires were hopscotching all over the park due to cinders being carried by the wind. The fires were even jumping meadows and rivers, the Park's natural fire breaks. Thus with no established fire front, it was impossible to predict the route of the fire's path. The Park Service and Fire Fighters did the best that could be done in a very bad situation. We are very fortunate the wisdom of the Park Service prevailed.

At night the fires "lay down", that is, they burn slower because there is less heat and wind to keep them moving. It was at night many attempts were also made to control the fires movement. A fire retardent was mixed with water and dropped by aircraft over the path where the fire was predicted to go. Sophisticated planes with hi-tech sensors flew over the areas at night to find the hot spots. Hot spots were the areas at the front of the fires where they wanted to drop the retardant. It has been told these sensor pilots did not always talk with the Park Service before reporting the hot spots to the other pilots with the retardant to be dropped from their planes. If they had talked with the Park Service, they could have been told some of the hot spots they were picking up on their radar screens were actually thermal features, like geysers. This lack of communication is one reason a lot of retardant was wasted and dropped on areas such as geyser basins!

The efforts of the Park Service and the Fire fighters saved the Old Faithful Inn and many other places of national importance. (A special thanks to Bob Barbee and Dan Sholly.)

We understand now the fires were not necessarily a sad event. They were just another event of Nature.

The first snowfall in October finally put the fires out.

My Summer

This book is as much about the summer I spent in Yellowstone as anything. I want very much for this narrative to be a personal journal.

The people I met were incredible: Tatiana, an All-American Volleyball player from Lake Erie College, Rachel, a business student from England, Kirtie, a pre-med student at Princeton, Matt from Boston College. This is how I spent my summer, spending every day talking with these and many other remarkable people. I hope, after you complete this book, you will want to either visit or work in Yellowstone.

◆◆◆

Any time I talked with a Park employee, I would start the conversation by saying, "I am Clint Wilkes and I'm writing a book about the people working in Yellowstone." I never attempted or planned anything covert. Every question and answer I received was "on the record."

Several years ago a reporter from *"Rolling Stone"* magazine went undercover, posing as a high school student. The result was an article in the magazine and the movie, *"Fast Times At Ridgemont High"*. It would have been very easy for me to have been incognito all summer.

Jodi and Clint eating Pizza at "Mountain High Pizza Pie". Jodi graduated from Georgia and owns her own business in Jackson Hole.

I had no intention of writing about gossip I heard. I planned to write about the subjects which I felt directly involved working in Yellowstone. Whatever someone does privately has nothing to do with a summer job in Yellowstone.

I also never tried to "party" with the college age employees. I did become friends with a lot of college student employees.

My age and my demeanor were both assets in working on this book. I would hope I developed a sense of trust with everyone I interviewed.

I also used my discretion in describing scenes I saw. If someone was scatfaced on Firewater in a bar I happen to be in, I did not put that scene in the book. Anything someone told me when they were blitzed is not in this book.

Do I want to sell books? Yes, I do. But that is not, believe it or not, why I am writing this. I want as many college students as possible to work in Yellowstone for a summer.

If you bought a book and you have a friend who can not afford a book, please loan them yours. Or if you will send me the address of the library for your school I will send the library a free copy of this book.

I am very happy with my life. I have wonderful friends and the best support from my family anyone could ask for. My neice, my two god-daughters and my nephews are all a real blessing.

Imagine having all of this and then coming up with a means to support yourself while spending your summers in Yellowstone!

I spent a couple of weeks in Alabama with my parents before departing for Yellowstone. I flew from Birmingham back to Austin on May 1st. I planned to spend a few days with my best friends Jean and Jay in Dallas before starting the drive to Yellowstone.

I had already discussed and made plans with my god-daughter April to put her picture on the cover of this book. We had also planned for her to fly out to Yellowstone and work with me on the preparation of this manuscript. Her picture on the cover is to let women college students be aware they have the opportunity to work in Yellowstone.

April is on a ballet scholarship at S.M.U. and would have only been able to work with me in the Park for a few weeks. She already had several ballet training seminars set to attend.

All of these plans were made before she broke her leg!

We knew the injury would heal, but to remain a dancer would require extensive therapy. Her summer was now planned.

Yellowstone would not be a part of it.

It was an easy decision for me to make to leave April's picture on the cover. She had every intention of working with me in the Park. She had actually broken her leg in class on a most routine jump she had made a thousand times before. This was not her fault.

April did serve as a consultant on this book. Every week I sent her a disk to review what I had written. Her help was invaluable!

I love April and her sister Bonnie very much. I look forward to Bonnie working with me when she gets to college in a few years.

April will be with me as I do the revised editions of this book over the years. She was with me in spirit this year.

◆◆◆

Like will happen with most of you, I did not know anyone when I first arrived in Yellowstone. I had come up in January to work on the chapter *Winter in Yellowstone*. I met a most remarkable group of employees. I looked forward to seeing them again during the Summer. Many of them I did see as they were now working all over the Park during the Summer.

I was also meeting new employees for the first time. Several hundred times during the summer I would walk up to an employee and say, "hello, my name is Clint Wilkes and I am writing a book on the people of Yellowstone." The response was always positive. Even those people who had only been in the Park for a short time had already fallen in love with this place.

I also made many new friends. I enjoyed being a "tour guide" and taking people around to see the wonders of Yellowstone.

During May, when only part of the Park was open, I made a few ventures outside the Park. I drove to Bozeman and spent a night. I got up early the next morning and drove sixty miles to visit the Montana Tech campus in Butte, Montana. Butte is a mining town built on the side of a hill.

After lunch that same day I drove the seventy miles to Helena, the capitol of Montana. I played tourist both that afternoon and the next morning in the town and in the State Capitol building. Inside the impressive Capitol building, the Paxson western paintings and the Russell western painting are alone worth the visit. The Russell is on the wall behind the Speaker's desk in the House chambers. The Paxsons are in the House lobby.

The Clint Wilkes Original College Guide to a Summer Job in Yellowstone

The Author

I knew when I started planning my summer in Yellowstone I would take off several days to drive to Colorado Springs. I have wanted to tour the Air Force Academy ever since I met and became friends with General Robinson "Robbie" Risner and his beautiful wife, Dot.

In the early 1980s, I worked with Texas State Senator Mike Richards, from Sugar Land. This was during a time when America was first becoming aware of the devastating effect drugs were having on our society. The Texas legislature passed laws called *"The Texans War On Drugs"*. General Risner was in charge of a program to make Texans aware of the drug problem. When the legislature adjourned I became one of the *"War On Drugs"* speakers. I travelled throughout Texas for over two years speaking to civic groups about the legislation we had passed and the dangers of illegal drugs. During this time I developed a strong admiration and, fortunately for me, a friendship with Dot and Robbie.

They are both remarkable people. It is my opinion that in the dictionary under *"hero"*, it should simply say, *"Robinson Risner"*.

General Risner was an Ace fighter pilot in the Korean War. During the Vietnam War, he was shot down and captured in North Vietnam and held prisoner for seven and a half years. His book on the experience, *"The Passing Of The Night"*, was a world-wide best seller.

His skills as a fighter pilot are without comparison. The Air Force gives an award each year to the top fighter pilot to graduate from its fighter pilot school at Nellis Air Force base in Las Vegas. That award is called the *"Risner Trophy"*. This is the only military trophy ever to be named after a person who is still alive. The pilot gets a replica of the trophy. An original of the trophy is on display at the Air Force Academy in Colorado Springs.

This dictionary I mentioned before should have *"Dot Risner"* as the definition of two words, *"grace"* and *"charm"*. If anyone in the world is more remarkable than Robbie, it would be Dot! This couple is so much fun to be around! Dot has a terrific sense of humor which I am constantly putting to the test, usually much to my chagrin. Try as I may to get in one of my good-natured "zingers" on Dot, it is not most of the time but all of the time she will get in an even better and always funnier "zinger" on me.

The best one I remember was one evening I was to meet Dot and Robbie in Austin for dinner at the *Oasis*, a restaurant famous for its sunset views. It sits on a mountain overlooking Lake Travis. On the way out to the *Oasis*, I passed one of Austin's many famous country western nightclubs. A place you could catch me if *"Asleep At The Wheel"* were performing, but a place which I am sure would not ever be visited by Robbie or Dot.

This one had a name like "Bad Bill's Bronco Bustin' Bar". They had a sign out front which said, "Mini Skirt Contest Tonight". In my mind I prepared the "zinger". I only had to wait for the exact timing.

As we finished our meal and waited on dessert, I prepared my perfect sentence. I could not wait to see the look on Dot's face as I "zinged" her. At the precise moment, I looked at Robbie and said, "Robbie, when we finish dinner why don't we take Dot home and you and I will go to Bad Bill's. They're having a mini-skirt contest tonight." Without blinking an eye, Dot looked at me and said, "Clint, where did you find a mini-skirt that would fit you?"

I am now out of the "zinger" business!

I talked to Robbie several weeks before I left Austin. He told me he would be in Colorado Springs for a Air Force reunion in mid-May. He said he would have some free time the evening he arrived. I picked him up at the airport and we went to dinner. I also met him for coffee the next morning.

I toured the Air Force Academy later that morning. The entire complex is awesome. I was especially proud to see the statue of General Risner in the Air Garden.

◆◆◆

I was also indirectly responsible for my friend, Texas Supreme Court Justice Bob Gammage, getting his son, Robert, a job working in the Grand Tetons several years ago. Robert was finishing his first yeat of college which did not get out until mid-June. I mentioned to Bob how I thought Robert would enjoy working in the Yellowstone area. I also told Bob I thought all the jobs might be taken but he could call the Park and find out.

I saw Bob a couple of days later, and he told me Robert would be leaving in a few days to live in Moose, Wyoming and to work in the Tetons.

I was amazed at what I had done! Bob then told me the rest of the story. Bob said he was thinking about Robert getting a summer job when it occured to him he had served on the Interior Committee in Congress with Manual Lujan, who was then the Secretary of the Interior for President Bush.

Bob had called the Interior Department in Washington and had explained to Secretary Lujan how he was looking for a job for Robert. A couple of hours later he got a phone call back from Mr Lujan, who told him of an immediate opening in the Tetons working with the Forest Service.

I do not think Robert was real happy at first. He was earning about five dollars an hour, spending all day in the wilderness. He grew to love it and is now in the Army Combat Engineer Corps where he spends most of his time on maneuvers in the wilds of the world.

To get an application for the National Forest Service in the Grand Tetons write: National Forest Service, Moose, Wy.

I first met Bob Gammage as he was in the middle of his first term in Congress. He had been elected to the Texas State House of Representatives soon after he had graduated from The University of Texas Law School. After one term he was elected to the Texas Senate.

The incumbent Congressman resigned to take a Presidential appointment, and Bob was soon elected to Congress. His political career was zooming!

When I met him, we developed an immediate bond. Since I had gotten both my B.A. and M.B.A. on the G.I.

Bill, I was older than many of the other volunteers. I was soon serving as Bob's driver when he would come in from Washington on weekends. *(Years later, Bob and I would take Negotiations together at Harvard Law School.)*

During the next year, our friendship grew enormously. Even though I enjoyed the time I spent with Bob while he was in Congress, I never remembered him laughing or doing anything to have fun except on a very rare occasion.

With election night upon us, I fully expected a landslide victory. I was also mentally preparing myself for the Washington job offer which was sure to come the following day.

I knew very little about Texas politics.

Bob had run a textbook positive campaign. He never stooped into the mud and vicious personal attacks our opponent bombarded us with every day. As the returns came in during the night, the vote count was razor thin close. At midnight we knew we had lost by a few hundred votes.

The staff and volunteers were devastated. I, along with the other women and men, was crying and angry. We believed some voting irregularities had occurred and were confident a recount would give us the victory we felt we had earned.

Bob had been in an office with his family for about an hour when he called the staff in for our last campaign meeting.

The man who addressed us then was more impressive than the man I had worked so diligently for during the past year. First, he said we should all join in congratulating our opponent. Those campaign staff members who had taken leave from Washington to work on the campaign should work closely with our opponent's staff to insure a smooth transition. He also stated there would be no mention from anyone in his office about a recount. The election was over!

During the next years, I spent much time with Bob. He was actually a fun person to be around. I will never forget going to a country western club with him and watching him dance with his wife. I had no idea he could have fun.

After his family, the law was Bob's true love. Four years after leaving Congress, he was elected to a Judgeship on the Texas Court of Appeals. He was reelected without opposition. When he ran for the Texas Supreme Court, he won with one of the largest percentages of all the candidates running statewide.

Today, Bob is one of the most popular members of the Supreme Court. I have lunch with him at least once or twice a week, when I am home in Austin, at the T.E.C. cafeteria. This is Bob's favorite, and one of the most unique places to eat in Austin. Bob eats there almost every day. You will usually find several of his staff seated with him at our usual table. The best days are when Charlie from Bob's office or Ray, our very good friend, can join us. For me, I love the T.E.C. cafeteria. The food is delicious, plus Frank, the owner, will join us when he can.

In 1984, I returned to my home state of Alabama to run for the United States Senate. The incumbent was Howell Heflin. I never made any derogatory personal attacks on Senator Heflin. Senator Heflin is a true Southern gentleman.

What can you gain by losing? The obvious answer is nothing. This may be obvious, but it is not true. Everything I accomplished to prepare to run for the Senate, I still have. I still have my education, my family and my friends. I was invited to The White House and I got to meet President Reagan. I was on television, radio, and the front page of every newspaper in Alabama with positive stories.

I can honestly say to myself, I gave it my best shot. Am I disappointed I lost? I was then. I could not be any happier than I am now. I do not think I would be where I am now if I had run a vicious smear campaign against a fine man like Howell Heflin. I also know I would not have been satisified if I had won by resorting to anything less than the type of campaign I ran.

I will be doing a book tour. I would love to speak about Yellowstone on your campus. Write to the address used to order books and someone from my office will get in touch with your school.

This venture to Yellowstone is a big risk. I think college students will be interested. I hope you are.

I do know I will always come back to Yellowstone.

SO LONG PARDNER. SEE YOU IN YELLOWSTONE.

YES, please send me ____ copies of **The Clint Wilkes Original College Guide to a Summer Job in Yellowstone.**

_____
NAME

_____
ADDRESS

_____
CITY   STATE   ZIP

I ENCLOSE $12.95 PLUS $3.00 SHIPPING AND HANDLING, TOTAL $15.95 PER COPY.

Send this order form to:
Clint Wilkes Yellowstone Guide
P.O. Box 192
Pinson, Alabama 35126